INFORMATION
AND THE MODERN
CORPORATION

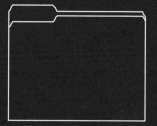

INFORMATION AND THE MODERN CORPORATION

JAMES W. CORTADA

The MIT Press | Cambridge, Massachusetts | London, England

For information on quantity discounts, email special_sales@mitpress.mit.edu

Set in Chaparral Pro by the MIT Press. Printed and bound in the United States of America.

Library of Congress Cataloging-in-Publication Data

Cortada, James W.
Information and the modern corporation / James W. Cortada.
p.   cm. — (MIT Press Essential Knowledge)
Includes index.
ISBN 978-0-262-51641-9 (pbk. : alk. paper) 1. Knowledge management.
2. Corporations. 3. Information resources management. 4. Information technology—Management. I. Title.
HD30.2.C6695 2011
658.4'038—dc22

2011005885

10   9   8   7   6   5   4   3   2   1

CONTENTS

SERIES FOREWORD

The MIT Press Essential Knowledge series presents short, accessible books on need-to-know subjects in a variety of fields. Written by leading thinkers, Essential Knowledge volumes deliver concise, expert overviews of topics ranging from the cultural and historical to the scientific and technical. In our information age, opinion, rationalization, and superficial descriptions are readily available. Much harder to come by are the principled understanding and foundational knowledge needed to inform our opinions and decisions. This series of beautifully produced, pocket-sized, soft-cover books provides in-depth, authoritative material on topics of current interest in a form accessible to nonexperts. Instead of condensed versions of specialist texts, these books synthesize anew important subjects for a knowledgeable audience. For those who seek to enter a subject via its fundamentals, Essential Knowledge volumes deliver the understanding and insight needed to navigate a complex world.

Bruce Tidor
Professor of Biological Engineering and Computer Science
Massachusetts Institute of Technology

After over 60 years of using computers, we have almost forgotten why we use them. People in nearly every country in the world have been too busy spending nearly $4 trillion a year acquiring and using information technologies to think about that. Every *Fortune* 1,000 firm is an extensive user of the technology, but we all know that "everyone" uses computers. It is why people in almost all walks of life are comfortable with such notions as the Information Age, the New Economy, and the Networked Economy or Age. While we have been infatuated with the latest i-gadgets from Apple, with what Google is doing, and with buying and selling on eBay, something else has been going on in the shadows.

That "something else" has been the fundamental transformation of whole firms and industries into giant information-processing engines. Instead of just "bending metal" to make products, most employees in a modern factory have evolved into knowledge workers. At an IBM plant in 1950, one would have seen hundreds if not thousands of workers wiring computers. Today less than 20 percent of the workers in a computer plant make anything; the rest are accountants, supply-chain supervisors, quality-control specialists, production supervisors, managers, analysts, computer scientists, and engineers. Banks do not have as much cash in their vaults and branches as they did in earlier years; instead, they have digital files that say they have large amounts of money, and they are managing information about how much a particular person or account has, not physically moving coins and paper from one pile to another. And so it goes in one industry after another: hundreds of millions of people working with information. They can do this reasonably well thanks to the existence of computers. Most commentators on information focus on the computers rather than on information, facts, and data.

The purpose of this book is to describe, indeed highlight, the role of information in the modern corporation, with only a tip of the hat to information technologies. People collect, analyze, and use information to do their work, to gain insights, to make more informed decisions, and even to share those roles and decision-making capabilities with machines, some of which are computers and some of which have computers built into them. The main theme of this book is that information—rather than information technology—is the fundamental building material of the modern enterprise, and that its use now defines the activities of firms far more than we might have imagined even 20 years ago. Most workers in medium-size and large companies are information purveyors, information junkies, and knowledge workers. This book is about them and their work.

People collect, analyze, and use information to do their work, to gain insights, to make more informed decisions, and even to share those roles and decision-making capabilities with machines, some of which are computers and some of which have computers built into them.

In this book I look at how information flows around and is used in enterprises more than at what information technology (IT) does. Yet it must be acknowledged that computing has shaped what information there is, how it is used, and what its consequences are. Information technology and the information it handles are co-dependent. But not all information sits in a computer; a great deal resides between the ears of millions of people, or on paper. I provide a quick tour through many parts of a corporation, demonstrating the existence and use of information, explaining why and how it is used, and ultimately addressing the role of information, the *style* in which we work today, which is rather new and still evolving. Along the way, I suggest implications and make suggestions on how best to deal with information in both strategic and tactical terms.

My goal in this brief book is to raise the reader's consciousness about the importance of information and how its central role shapes our work. For example, when we describe things today, we no longer use adjectives such as *great* or *pretty good*; instead we quantify how great or pretty good something is in numerical terms, using percentages, odds of happening, or the old standbys ROI (return on investment) and Six Sigma. Thus, how we make decisions has changed from just gut feel and experience to a greater reliance on empirical evidence, most notably numbers.

The argument this book proposes, put simply, is that information is being elevated back to its former prominence, a privileged position that was overtaken for a while by the glamour of IT. Now that it is everywhere and everyone has it, IT is mundane. It is how "things are done," no big deal, although IT innovations continue to create exciting and often profoundly important new business opportunities and ways to help run firms of all sizes. With more than 30 years' experience behind me working with IT and information in corporations, I am convinced that if you know more about information as a topic, as a tool, and as a way of thinking and doing, you can leverage it better than you do today by design and not by accident. Observe your behavior, learn from it, and you will do things smarter.

Because we have to view information in a holistic manner to appreciate its presence and its role in the modern enterprise, this book is a high-speed tour through the main activities of the modern enterprise, introducing its presence and its mission. I discuss implications, and I conclude with a preview of future developments. This book is not graced with charts, graphs, numerous examples, case studies, and endnotes—information baubles—because it is not a monograph. Rather, it is an essay—an extended conversation—highlighting the role of information. If the reader accepts my argument, there will be plenty of time to read the more involved monographs on specific aspects of information with a context by which to appreciate how it all fits together. Because I refer to various surveys and studies that I and my colleagues at IBM have conducted on the modern role of information, management, and the modern enterprise, the reader may want to probe some of the points made in this book more deeply. To that end, I direct the reader to a website at which about 200 reports can be found. The address is http://www.ibm.com/iibv.

I owe a deep debt of gratitude to my colleagues at the IBM Institute for Business Value, who taught me much about how the modern enterprise works and continues to evolve. Without their insights the book would have been difficult to write. I want to also thank the MIT Press for showing faith in my work by publishing this book. In particularly, I am deeply grateful to my editor, Marguerite Avery, for helping me shape this project into a practical conversation about the world we all live in today. I found the suggestions of several anonymous reviewers reassuring and useful—many thanks to them for investing their time in this book. Any weaknesses or errors are of my own doing. The views expressed are my own, and do not necessarily reflect those of IBM or the MIT Press.

The search for insight into the role of information in the modern enterprise is a journey. Thank you for sharing the trip as we collectively learn to live in the Information Age.

WORKING THE DIGITAL WAY

The way people work in large and small enterprises has evolved in response to the availability of more and different information over the past 20 years, and as a result of the increased number of information technologies that individuals can use to collect, analyze, control, and use data. Today people use more information to make decisions and to take action than ever before. That way of working represents a *style* of going about our work that can be described as digital and information-intensive. That style affects the activities and the thinking of managers, their staffs, and even their smart machines. This chapter introduces this new style of working.

Information—Today's Source of Power and Decisions

Data and information seem to be everywhere. We read that a laptop computer can hold as much information as an academic library filled with books. Reporters, sociologists, TV journalists, and academics comment on the amount of information in the world and on how it is increasing faster than ever before.

Data, information, knowledge, and wisdom all are needed by people to do their work and to live their lives. Corporations are great collectors and users of data. (That is essentially the biggest task of a financial institution or a school.) Data come in many forms and are moved about the enterprise by all its employees, business partners, and customers. Data are facts, such as names or numbers. If sensors are collecting these, there are electronic impulses when something happens or when something moves. Budgets and spreadsheets—filled with data—are the raw materials of modern work. Information is slightly different in that it combines various data to say something that the data alone can't say. For instance, data on our spending habits tell us about our financial behavior and about our patterns of expenditures—that is information, not just groups of unrelated numbers. Understanding the history of the relations between a customer and a seller over a period of years is also information, and can include narratives of past events, judgments about the behavior of individuals, and facts (data) on business volumes and transactions, all often in some organized way, such as by way of a PowerPoint presentation or a written document. In both instances, data and information are explicit

Then there is wisdom: the ability to make sense of data, information, and knowledge in ways that are relevant to an organization.

because they are specific, and, although they may have some value judgments associated with them, they stand alone.

Knowledge is more complicated than data or information because it combines data, information, and experiences from logically connected groups of facts (such as budget data from a department) with things that have no direct or obvious connection (such as previous jobs and experiences). Because experiences and even subconscious associations with other data occur, we call this *tacit knowledge*. One hears this expressed as "experience" or "gut feel," but also increasingly as "knowledge." Acquiring and using knowledge is the ultimate objective of data and information, because it can lead to trusted insight. That set of combinations is also the highest goal because it is aggregated, which means it can be applied to making decisions and taking action. It is increasingly being organized and managed in structured ways. That is why chapter 2 is devoted to knowledge management.

Then there is wisdom: the ability to make sense of data, information, and knowledge in ways that are relevant to an organization. We expect a senior leader in an enterprise to have wisdom based on decades of working in an industry. But wisdom can occur all over a firm if people have the ability to "connect the dots" and to answer such questions as "So What?" and "What does it mean?" You can instruct someone to collect data and information before making a decision, and you can instruct someone to use data and information to track performance, but you can't automate or teach wisdom.

Data, information, and knowledge have become so embedded in the operations of the modern enterprise and so visible that their use and their management constitute the essential work of the modern worker, especially in industries in which people do what used to be called "office work." Wisdom exists in every organization, often is hidden, sometimes can be seen in the activities of an individual, but is channeled into work in an organized manner.

Because information—the aggregation of data and the prerequisite for knowledge—is the most important asset (or, as some think, tool) available to the modern worker, its effective use brings power and promotions to individuals, enabling people at all levels in an organization to measure results and improve performance in a fact-based manner rather than by "gut feeling" or impression. It gives courage to management to make important decisions about who to hire, what products to develop (and when), and what markets to pursue. It is the scientific method of learning about one's environment applied to an enterprise and taking action on the basis of what it teaches us. That style of running an organization may represent the biggest fundamental change in the nature of work and management to have occurred in the past 60 years. Without the rise of information as a valued way of influencing our work, information technologies would be less useful and would be used by fewer people. That is why information outranks IT.

The availability of ever-increasing amounts of information in useful and manageable forms has contributed to the more formal organization of work that now is evident across all functions in the modern enterprise. The notion of work as collecting tasks into processes, first introduced in the 1920s, came into full deployment after it became routine and convenient to use information to document transactions, organize tasks, and assess performance—which happened during the second half of the twentieth century. It was the availability of information that made work more organized. It is why much of the discussion in this short book is about the existence and the use of information within work processes, such as supply-chain management, product development, customer relations, and sales.

Computers Are Everywhere

Today anyone who works in a mid-size to large enterprise anywhere in the world uses a computer. That is correct: anyone. Most individuals may not realize how true that is, because computers may be embedded in equipment they use: mobile or land-line telephones, the vehicles they drive (all of which have microprocessors), laptops, terminals, the photocopiers and coffee machines in their offices, the robotic painting equipment in an automobile factory. Automated teller machines and traffic lights work because of computers; so do elevators and ID-badge readers. These technologies are the visible side of information flowing through an enterprise. There are so many such technologies that nobody can tally them up anymore. But what is important to acknowledge is that they increasingly make up the visible part of the skeletal structure of the modern enterprise through which data and information flow to individuals. This often occurs in highly integrated and choreographed ways which people then use as part of their work. In the process, they convert data and information into knowledge and wisdom—two conversions not yet done by computers.

Collections of computers are not simply jumbles of technologies; they actually have formed quasi-organized structures that, if one recognizes them, can be tuned to optimize the gathering, analysis, and flow of information. They are part of a process of managing information that goes back hundreds of years to the days when government archives, intelligence operations, schools, and research centers depended on paper. Today the dependence is increasingly on digital electronics.

All enterprises have centers of data warehousing. Large enterprises' data centers are stocked with large mainframe computers (called *servers* today), which are linked to smaller mainframes, then to terminals and laptop computers through wired and wireless telecommunications networks, and to intelligent sensing devices, such as motion sensors, security cameras, and devices that guide robotic forklifts in warehouses. Some types of data, such as those produced by accounting and by financial reporting, are centralized in these centers. (Enterprises are required by law to provide composite economic views of their business results.) Others are physically housed in factories to handle the gathering, analysis, and dissemination of information related to all the work done there, or in a regional headquarters (e.g., of a national banking corporation). At the individual level there is the terminal or the laptop computer—wired or wireless, in a company's building, in a home office, or on the road.

There are at least two other networks of computers that people use in the course of their work today. The first is a telephone network, which has three parts. The first is the traditional wired telephone, normally managed through a central system or outsourced to a national telephone company. The second is the wireless cell phone, which may be owned by or issued to a worker. Wireless phones are increasingly able to perform work that before could only be done on a terminal or a laptop computer, such as finding directions, checking e-mail, making travel arrangements, and reading data files. "Smart phones" serve as platforms for the delivery of functions (information) in various forms (music, voice, text, images, video), individually or in combination. Finally, there are myriad other devices people use for personal and professional purposes, to access increasingly the Internet. The most widely used include BlackBerrys, iPads, and GPS devices.

External and internal to the enterprise is the ubiquitous Internet. It operates as both an external conduit for data coming in or leaving the enterprise and an internal closed network for just moving information inside an organization. Of the 7 billion people on Earth, more than 2 billion use it, and a billion more are about to gain access. It is rapidly becoming humankind's data and communications backbone. As this chapter was being written, the Internet was handling more than 22 exabytes of data at once. An exabyte is a quintillion (10^{18}) pieces of data. All the printed matter on Earth amounts to about 5 exabytes. In short, the Internet is a big infrastructure for housing data, but it isn't the only one. Many IT experts expect that the volume of information on the Internet will double in a few years and then double again before this book goes out of print. Data moving through the Internet come in and out of the enterprise's infrastructure of computers and communications. When you bank via the Internet, or when you look at an online trade magazine as part of your job, using a laptop computer issued to you by your company, the two are merged.

Machines also rely on the Internet and the collection of computers in an enterprise. Many devices that monitor activities collect information and send it directly to computers without human intervention, as when digitally connected meters in an oil pipe tell a firm how much crude oil has passed through the pipe on its way to a refinery. Video cameras at road intersections send data to computers to issue fines to those who run red lights, then track payment of the fines. Radio-frequency identification (RFID) tags on pallets of products tell modern armies and Wal-Mart that specific materiel or merchandise has arrived at some destination. Such devices are expected to outnumber human users of the Internet by 10 to 1 by the year 2020.

The important insight one can draw from computing is that the technology has become an integral part of organized work activities (often called *processes*) and unorganized tasks. How work is optimized often involves resolving questions about what data and information is needed and who or what will collect it, assess it, store it, make decisions reliant on it, and take actions. The technology allows one to move more quickly, or differently, on the basis of four things: the shape and size of the digital technologies, their costs relative to those of other options (including older computing devices), their ease of use, and the value of the information they handle. Decades ago, all these decisions and uses were done by humans and were human-centered. While it may seem obvious that human-centered and human are the same, they are not. As IT systems acquire authority to make decisions and then to alter data, decisions and work are transforming to meet the needs of software tools, stepping away from being human-centered in the process. Emerging trends of not being human-centered include sub-second decision making based on data coming in quicker than humans can process them and data consisting of electronic pulses rather than human language or notation. But as new devices and software become available, each of these four facets of the technology's life is increasingly determined and influenced by other machines, all of which have computational capabilities. This means that they can collect, use, and store data and information from computers, and can make decisions based on it.

All the World Is a Collection of Processes

It is no accident that an automobile company can take 6,000 employees at one factory, add millions of parts, and produce 200,000–300,000 vehicles, each with thousands of parts, in a timely and cost-effective manner. Across all industries, and only since the 1960s, management as a whole has come to recognize that the vast majority of work should be viewed as collections of processes, although many managers did so as early as the 1910s as a result of the development of the mass-production method of manufacturing goods, such as the Model T Ford. These are tasks that are done repeatedly, and today most tasks (work) fit that description.

Management learned that by viewing work through the lens of processes they could improve the speed at which work was done and the quality (accuracy) of the tasks, and in the process lower costs. Integral to that way of viewing work is information that documents every step of the way for employees working in the process; tracks progress made in quality, cost, speed, and exceptions to the work flow; and provides insights into how processes can be improved or be reengineered. A process-centric view of work gave employees and management deeper insights as to what was going on and, in the case of the automobile industry, how to organize in bigger groups to make more complex products, or offer a greater variety of services.

In addition, collecting information on performance made it possible to improve these processes, and that meant applying statistics (often called metrics). At a minimum these always involved numerical calculations of performance. By 2000, it seemed everyone was tracking the quality of performance or applying Six Sigma measures, without a mathematician in sight. And that was the major revolution in the role of information in the modern enterprise, a major event of the 1970s: collecting data and information about work flows—processes—as a routine part of everyone's work. The gurus of "quality management" taught us how to do that. Machines now have metrics-collecting software embedded in them, and today most employees think of work in process-centric terms. The language of working people, whatever their level of education or their background, is heavily laced with words and concepts that are statistical, numerical, and often mathematical.

Well-managed processes have clearly defined owners. Those individuals may also "own" a department and employees, but process owners control the people, computers, parts, and mission or objectives of a process. Processes have defined borders, just as in earlier decades departments did. Properly run processes have all their work steps and measures documented, with control points, measurements of performance, and steps that can be taken to manage natural deviations from expectations. When management and employees think about optimizing work, they think about improving the performance of processes, often with specific numerical or factual targets in mind—in other words, with articulated expectations arrived at through analysis and understanding of information about existing or anticipated work processes. *Fortune* 1,000 companies adhere to these; their suppliers, usually smaller firms, are forced to do the same as extensions of their customers; even small independent enterprises increasingly do that. Process-centric management is now universal.

Analytics—the New Way to Insight

Fact-based understanding of how processes work and how they are performing has been extended to new levels of applications. The terms "analytics" and "business intelligence" now are widely used in the modern enterprise to indicate increased use of numbers, statistics, quantitative analysis, modeling, forecasting, and predictions, all to do what started with process management: to improve the quality of decision making and to help manage multiple activities (processes). Analytics is being applied in increasingly varied activities of an enterprise: determining what products to develop and sell, linking to and assessing financial services, monitoring environmental effects of a company's activities, tracking sales of consumer goods, inventing new drugs and medical procedures, and so on.

Manual and software-based analytical tools are increasingly pervasive in departments and divisions of mid-size and larger firms. These tools are used to generate routine reports, to establish one-off accounts that probe batches of data (usually already in numerical form in a computer), to model analyses, to define scenarios, to quantify costs, to document benefits and features of scenarios, and to predict outcomes. Analytics has gone mainstream in the daily affairs of people because it gives management a greater base of facts on which to take action by reducing risk of the unknown. The use of analytics has a long history, however. In the 1970s, when personal computers were first available, the most widely used application was analysis requiring the use of spreadsheet software. It remains the iconic tool of analytics, with a 35-year history of use by hundreds millions of people. Many of these people now do this kind of work using large mainframes and far more sophisticated software tools in addition to their humble laptops and PCs.

Analytics was imposed on top of statistical analysis as scientific, economic, and business research increasingly made it clear that data (largely *numerical* data), when structured and analyzed using the discipline of many mathematical algorithms and statistical tools developed in the past 50 years, and with software available since the early 2000s, were of practical use in making more accurate judgments and better decisions. As the tools also made predictions regarding future quality of products and scope of sales, that capability further encouraged a generation of managers raised on science, engineering, statistics, mathematics, and disciplined business managerial practices to use such tools.

In addition to understanding competitors and locating opportunities to drive down costs and to increase profits or revenues, software analytical tools are beginning to help enterprises define and support strategic initiatives, such as defining and measuring competitive distinctiveness without emotion, corporate political agenda, personal bias, or ignorance of a subject. One aspect of the ability of software, computers, and data is the capability to coordinate (or integrate) larger bodies of information than a human being can. In the 1970s the Soviets tried to model their entire economy; they failed because there were too many moving parts. Today the Russians still can't model their entire economy down to the level of detail required to run it, but almost every *Fortune* 1,000 company routinely models various lines of business, understands its sets of customers, and makes decisions about what goods and services to offer, relying on analytics. Analytics is even why the price of an airplane ticket varies during the course of a week and even by the hour.

In some enterprises there are departments dedicated to doing this kind of analysis. Procter & Gamble is perhaps the best known of these enterprises, but most large companies routinely use such tools to understand their markets. Just as governments have centralized intelligence gathering, many divisions and departments of firms have experts in analytics (statistics) and other forms of data collection and analysis. Many widely used managerial constructs exist for setting up and managing such functions, often aligned with robust uses of IT, mathematics, and statistics, and many employees access them to study large bodies of data.

Business-oriented analytics is entering a new era of popularity, and is becoming pervasive. Companies use such tools widely across the firm, delegate more decision making to software, pay attention to earlier patterns and trends, flag variations from expected behavior, and present data in more insightful visual forms. When we add to this list more predictions and less reporting of mundane data, and, of course, expanded uses of data mining, we begin to see the emergence of intelligent automation of information management, not simply data handling.

Road Warriors—the New Normal Work Style

Nearly half of IBM's 400,000 employees don't work from 9 to 5, don't go to an IBM office every day, and often are "out of town." Their offices are anywhere. Their most important tools are laptop computers, cell phones, and good wireless connections. They live in a world of data, information, and knowledge. Their working world is about the glue that holds IBM and their clients' organizations together— expertise and an ability to apply it. These people include consultants, sales staff, auditors, accountants, IT gurus, software engineers, scientists, process engineers, and lawyers. They are like millions of workers in thousands of firms in approximately 200 industries.

As in other enterprises, it is not unusual for 10–80 percent of any corporation's staff to move about from one community to another, to be too familiar with airports, and to deal only with information. Their stock in trade is deep knowledge of something. They are continuously connected to their work, laboring for long hours and increasingly in short bursts of time as they multiprocess. These members of the modern corporation have their own nickname: "road warriors." This class of knowledge workers was made possible by cheap airplane tickets, outstanding education and training, laptop computers, the Internet, and broadband and wireless communications.

Their role was most importantly shaped by what they do. In the most advanced economies over the past 20 years, service industries have grown in importance as contributors to gross domestic product. Within enterprises, their contribution to generating revenue has grown too. A quick look at any recent IBM annual report shows that more than one-third of the company's revenues now come from people who use their brains, education, and methods of organizing data, information, and processes to support their clients through services and consulting, as do most of its competitors. This increased reliance on consultants is more than simply outsourcing or adding temporary staff to get over short-term increases in work, such as Christmas sales for retailers. This use of people is about running a modern enterprise in a structured, fact-based, almost quasi-scientific manner. This is knowledge work.

But the more important observation is that one does not have to be a "road warrior" to be part of what the modern enterprise is increasingly engaged in as creators, users, and protectors of information to create economic value for the enterprise. Most workers have such a role to play, even people we don't think of as knowledge workers, because they too have to collect data, learn from the data, measure performance against the data, and base decisions and actions on facts. That is why in the United States more than 75 percent of workers interact with computers and other digital devices regularly, why most industrial equipment collects data for users, and why the U.S. Department of Commerce now tracks the information sector, just as it used to track agriculture, manufacturing, and the service sector.

Implications

The network of information in the modern enterprise that has changed the work of employees and made organizations reliant on great amounts of data to function is expanding rapidly to include emerging information needs. Expanding areas of use include data about social and environmental conditions in which enterprises function and extended global connectivity tied to legal and social responsibilities. The volume of operational information is growing exponentially and in more granular forms than in the past as novel information comes into an organization from new sources, such as sensors, satellite images, video, and social networking sites on the Internet.

The style of working digitally is transforming from just relying on reporting about previous events (such as last month's sales) to presenting real-time operational data, although these kinds of changes are not yet as automatic or up to date as management now wants. Lack of adequate immediacy in presenting information is a problem that all surveys of information needs indicate that management is addressing, along with the problem of supply chains still too insular in their linkages to information in many departments and across multiple enterprises from suppliers to customers. These two problems come at a time when supply chains are increasingly participating in a renaissance in the collection and use of data and information about customers.

The new digital style of working in information-intensive enterprises includes the development of ways to identify gaps in information and tools for analysis that enhance previous practices in the collection and use of data. Additionally, there is a growing appetite to align business objectives with those of a larger community of stakeholders (such as suppliers, industry analysts, regulators) rather than only with those of management or stockholders. This alignment has to be buttressed with larger volumes of timely and well-organized data. The digital style also involves routinely assessing leading practices in information management, in benchmarking, and in data security.

KNOWLEDGE MANAGEMENT— MORE CORPORATE GLUE

If the modern corporation is largely a creator and a user of information, then facts and knowledge are among its most important assets, along with inventory and cash. If everyone in a company collects, stores, and uses information, then everyone in the company is, by definition, a manager of those assets. In reality, information is protected fiercely, while other facts are exposed like a hundred-dollar bill left on a desk or on the front seat of an automobile in full view. At one extreme, corporations guard some data with strident copyright practices and patent-management practices, locked rooms, and passwords; at the other extreme, someone leaves a laptop computer loaded with sensitive data on an automobile's front seat and then is chagrined to find the cherished Apple gone. Rarely does a corporation have a comprehensive approach to the management of its most used and most important asset: information.

Rarely does a corporation have a comprehensive approach to the management of its most used and most important asset: information.

What Is Knowledge Management?

The most obvious reason for sloppy management of an important corporate asset derives from the fact that most people (employees and management) do not consciously think about all the information they have as an asset that should be managed in an integrated fashion. Data mushroomed all over the enterprise in an *ad hoc* manner over the past 50 years in every conceivable place: a laptop, an employee's camera, a department's team room, a company-wide accounting system housed in a data center, the buildings of subcontractors and suppliers, data centers, and so on. Much paper-based information is also stored temporarily every day in trash cans before being thrown into unsecured garbage bins. Large quantities of data are transmitted wirelessly without encryption or any other form of security. On the other hand, road warriors and office-bound workers complain of having to use a dozen or more passwords to access their IT systems, but use unprotected wireless communications. In short, the management of the physical security of data is a mess. But one data-management practice is slowly moving from the halls of academia, where the nature and use of information is studied, into corporations. It is called *knowledge management* (KM).

To be sure, the phrase is a terrible one for corporations. Most business users of KM think of their facts as data or information, not knowledge, and think of data as comprising only material that is in a computer or on the Internet, typically only in one of three forms: spreadsheets, PowerPoint presentations, and text. Knowledge is less precise, yet the academics think of KM as comprising all of the above and more.

Simply stated, knowledge management is the identification, optimization, and active management of explicit or tangible informational assets (such as data physically stored in a computer or on a piece of paper) and tacit knowledge (information and insights residing largely in people's heads). Management of an explicit or tangible asset is optimized by making the data readily available to any employee who needs to have access to them in a cost-effective manner, whereas tacit knowledge is managed largely by creating communities of experts who collect, enhance, and share the knowledge. Explicit knowledge receives a great deal of attention from corporations. Tacit knowledge receives less attention, although that situation has been changing rapidly since 2000. The goal is to combine the two in some optimized fashion. Despite many attempts to do that, largely by using the techniques of explicit knowledge management, companies have not yet routinely succeeded. When success occurs, it is more by accident than by design, even though best practices are beginning to emerge and corporations are increasingly applying them.

Knowledge Management's Role Today

Knowledge management as an overt activity in corporations dates from the mid 1990s, though academics have discussed its possibilities for several decades. By the end of the twentieth century, various surveys of the *Business Week* Global 1,000 and of the *Fortune* 1,000 firms suggested that 70–80 percent had KM projects underway. In the United States, attendance at KM conferences by corporate officials surpassed 10,000. Subscriptions to KM newsletters were increasing steadily, too. Yet there are still too few best practices in KM, and many of the practices remain experimental and diffused.

Early efforts to manage information and knowledge involved the mining and the warehousing of data and the installation of various software tools for storing information (for instance, reports and data) for use by people on a team or by people who share common skills and interests. These various types of projects focused largely on explicit information. Anecdotal evidence suggests that formal efforts to leverage tactic knowledge are few and far between. A study done by the KM expert Laurence Prusak at the start of the new century cataloged about 120 such studies, so clearly this is a process that is just developing. But patterns of KM are emerging. Making knowledge visible is the most obvious. As the value of information in an enterprise is increasingly recognized, management finds ways to bring knowledge cohorts together, particularly in large enterprises that are scattered all over the world. Networks and virtual communities are being created in which experts regularly come together to share information, discuss issues, or work on company-wide problems. This is organized networking, leveraging virtual communities and information technologies and communications. Almost every large enterprise has such communities, some organized by management and some by like-minded experts on a subject. These specialized groups of experts hold workshops, train each other, share information, reports, books, and conversations, and present recorded material (for example, in podcasts).

A second set of activities involve the creation of knowledge infrastructures that facilitate the sharing of data, information, and access to experts on various subjects. The activities that receive the greatest amount of public and media attention are data mining, data analysis, analytics, use of multimedia tools, and use of network analysis software. Centers of competence, made up of groups of experts that other members of a firm can consult, are also popular.

A third set of initiatives—the most difficult—involves developing a corporate knowledge or learning culture with the intent of creating, codifying, sharing, and using information as part of the work everyone does. Normally, companies build IT infrastructures to facilitate the process, then encourage people to use it. Some companies, for example, will not reimburse an employee for travel expenses incurred in attending a conference until the employee has shared what he or she learned at the conference with a minimum number of fellow employees. But in general facilitation as a tool for dialogue concerns investing budget, allocating employee time to learn and share, deploying technologies to store and move information, and focusing management attention on the task.

Increasingly, employees and management alike are learning that it is essential to create communities of practice and to give them the networks and the time they need in order to learn from each other. That process results in knowledgeable people working on complex problems, suggesting innovations, and quickly and efficiently applying skills to the needs of customers and the enterprise at large.

In the early 2000s, the role of subject-matter experts (SMEs) became highly visible—particularly in the largest companies and in specialized consulting firms, where their job roles were defined and where their salaries often exceeded those of the managers to whom they reported. Some enterprises give their most highly skilled experts laboratories or time guaranteed for a defined number of years to work on some major knowledge-management or innovation project; others hold week-long conventions on their topics of expertise. Some SMEs teach part time at local universities. Firms are increasingly encouraging publication of their research and their best practices. Centers for development of thought-leadership materials are being established. Both were first done by high-technology firms and management consultancies; now such centers, and SME staffs, are proliferating in many industries.

Subject-matter experts are usually clustered around the kinds of work people do in a firm, or the products and services offered by the firm, following the model of most large management consultancies. An oil company will have organized communities of experts on drilling or on the transportation of petroleum products; a manufacturer of computer chips will have communities of experts knowledgeable about the physics and electronics of silicon wafers and other forms of chips and memory. Consultancies have communities of practice focused on tax services, cyber security, telecommunications, automotive fabrication techniques, and so on. The best SMEs are paid more than junior executives in many companies; indeed, some are promoted to the ranks of junior executives but without the burden of managing large staffs and budgets, so that they can, instead, apply and expand their knowledge and share it with the rest of the enterprise and with customers.

In short, knowledge management has rapidly gone from being an IT-centered domain of the Chief Information Officer, or having the function of retaining administrative records, to a diffused way of working across an enterprise. Some firms even appoint Chief Knowledge Officers (although that remains rare, largely because information now is diffused and affects nearly all employees, so that defining what a Chief Knowledge Officer does is nearly impossible).

Whether the information to be managed, nurtured, and added to using methods drawn from knowledge management's methods is tacit or explicit, the fundamental activity always is the routine processing of information within an organization, regardless of any awareness of KM. That is why it can be argued that the fundamental work of the modern enterprise is the collection and use of information. What individuals do with the information they work with is an *ad hoc*, informal form of KM. A manager who sets up folders on his laptop, a lawyer who lines her conference room with law books, and a salesman who keeps two cardboard boxes filled with product flyers in the trunk of his car are all practicing forms of KM (or, in the formal language of the academic expert, information management). As awareness of where and how people use an organization's information increases, these *ad hoc*, informal approaches to information management become subject to more formal controls. "Control" does not necessarily imply restrictions; rather, it refers to processes that optimize their use and protection. This move from information use to information management in all its variant forms and practices is increasingly becoming the domain of knowledge management. It should be obvious, therefore, that KM is not just about IT, online databases, or access to Google. Rather, KM goes to the heart of the culture, form, and activities of the enterprise, with important implications for the players in this drama.

Implications

One obvious implication is that the internal political power of a subject-matter expert has been increasing. There is now a large body of literature describing the "real" networks of power, which do not resemble traditional organization charts. For example, at IBM there are individuals who are recognized as having deep knowledge of a subject and who are often called upon by senior executives to render opinions that then affect decisions, trumping line management. When a firm finds itself in major trouble with the public or a customer, the informal KM process invariably kicks in, and the "real experts" in the enterprise come out of the shadows, or out of the depth of the organization, to offer quick, efficient, well-informed recommendations and make decisions.

Nurturing pools of experts, equipping them with necessary tools, creating a culture of information sharing and knowledge development, and knowing where to find experts in other parts of the enterprise when they are needed is the emerging role of knowledge management in the modern corporation.

Individual employees are increasingly exercising personal initiative to become experts, to link up with other fellow experts both inside and outside their firms, and to let it be known they are SMEs. They train and participate in their enterprise's skills certification programs and in other programs provided by national associations, also a form of KM. Credentialing has become an outward manifestation of the importance of information in the modern enterprise. One sees evidence of credentialing everywhere: "Dr." before a name on a business card, the initials of various certifications under a signature line in e-mail, a résumé that lists memberships in various associations, and a slowly emerging initiative on the part of some SMEs to demonstrate their cachet by publishing articles in trade and academic journals. Many SMEs appear on radio and television programs and make presentations at industry conferences. These activities represent increasingly recognized and valued uses of time, money, and technology. Experts already equipped with information, patents, and ways of the knowledge worker sometimes are hired; other experts are nurtured within the enterprise. But just as important are the conscious efforts and policies of a firm to recognize and exploit the fact that it is largely an institution that spends most of its time collecting and using information.

It is becoming more evident to management that deep understanding is required of the forces at work on the corporation and on its clients. As insight into these matters increases, concerns about what outputs are coming from IT are declining while interest in what workers do is increasing—a circumstance that is leading to a greater recognition that new skills will be needed by the enterprise. Just as accounting required accountants and financial experts, so too in KM, information management, or whatever else we want to call the methods of optimizing the use of data, facts, and insights. There are two kinds of information-management experts who are rarely hired into organizations to help manage information as an asset in any significant way: experts in library science and experts in computer science. Yes, librarians and computer experts (systems analysts, not programmers and PC jockeys). However, many corporations have librarians in their corporate libraries, and many have computer experts in their IT data centers. Both can be given more central roles in an enterprise.

The enterprise of the future will be a more information-intensive environment in which current uses of information are applied more formally and more rigorously. Progress toward that goal is already underway.

THE INFORMED SUPPLY CHAIN

The largest collections of activities (processes) in most corporations involve supply chains. No other group of activities requires as much information and coordination. No process for managing personnel and no process for accounting or financial tracking, for example, collects and uses data in such large quantities. A manufacturer of automobiles, a chain of retail dry-goods stores, a bank, and an insurance company all have supply chains with which to manage the flow of goods, supplies, activities, and expenses efficiently within the enterprise. The coordination of work and assets has been a subject of considerable managerial and academic attention for more than 100 years, and by 1990 it had a name: *supply chain*. When the supply chain is managed well, a corporation has more of an opportunity to lower its operating costs while improving efficiencies. For example, IBM's approach to procurement in the 1990s led to billions of dollars in cost savings relative to the previous supply chains, of which IBM had many; today it has one enveloping the entire corporation. As a bumper sticker put it in the 1990s, "everything is the supply chain."

What Are Supply Chains and Value Chains?

A supply chain is a sequence of activities that are coordinated in order to make and sell a product or to provide a service. A supply chain can begin, for example, with miners digging diamonds out of the ground, and can continue with a transportation company shipping the diamonds to diamond cutters, the cutters shipping them to jewelers to be set in engagement rings, and the jewelers selling the rings. Multiple activities have to be coordinated and tracked in a fairly routine way, and their costs accounted for, from the diamond pit to a lady's finger. Conversely, retailers have to understand the demand for rings, and that information has to be transmitted back through the supply chain to ensure that enough diamonds are dug out of the ground and that enough diamond cutters and jewelers are available to make rings. A supply chain usually includes planning, the resourcing of raw materials and components, manufacturing, delivery, sales, and post-sale services. Each step requires forecasting what is coming

As a bumper sticker put it in the 1990s, "everything is the supply chain."

and what is needed, and tracks what is done. Each step also has its own requirements. Planning encompasses synchronizing supply and demand, sourcing about fulfillment, manufacturing about production schedules and building; delivery encompasses scheduling, monitoring, and tracking; selling encompasses sales, merchandizing, and marketing; and services encompass training, customer interactions, and repairs.

Supply chains work because every step is accompanied by a body of information required to do the work. Information is collected in a routine manner, and is often shared from one step to another, often with participants in a different company (as in the case of a mining company and an ore-transportation firm), with multiple managers looking from left to right, from right to left, and up and down the supply chain to see how things are progressing. Information flows from one end of a supply chain to another, then back and forth. Thus, the market demand for rings is documented and reported to retailers and to jewelers and even further back to mining companies, along with results of how people performed their steps in the supply chain. Information also flows in the other direction, giving participants indications of where to improve efficiency. Because these steps have been extensively synchronized since the 1970s (thanks largely to computers and to an awareness of the power of synchronization of information and activities across departments, companies, even industries), a large body of best practices has emerged, most of which involve the collection and the management of ever-growing bodies of information.

Years before other industries manufacturing enterprises used concepts of supply chains. Today, companies in all industries do, including banks, hotel chains, consulting firms, and even departments within their own firms, such as procurement, training, and recruitment. Service supply chains often are more complex, and less understood, than those in manufacturing. Both types also include participants increasingly outside the formal borders of an enterprise: suppliers of components, government banks supplying cash to financial institutions, information vendors, and government officials, such as industry watchers, forecasters, and analysts that track the economy and changes in populations.

Variations of these chains emerge all the time. The most notable variation to arise in the past 20 years was the *value chain*, in which information on costs and returns on expenditures is collected for specific steps. This variation in the use of information has made it possible for enterprises to pinpoint potential areas of improvements in cost performance and potential sources of additional profits—for example, to identify expensive labor-intensive activities that could be outsourced to another firm or to a country with lower costs of labor, or automated, or simply discontinued.

The Evolution of Supply and Value Chains

Since about 1965, enterprises have found that using supply-chain views of their work made it possible either to drive down costs or to improve productivity in specific areas of their business. The most notable of the firms involved improved the acquisition and the use of raw materials and components and the rapid sale of finished inventory. For instance, by linking forecasts of what was needed, and exactly when it was needed, to customer requirements and to existing inventories, manufacturers reduced the cost of storing parts from weeks and months to days and hours, in what today is called *just-in-time inventory control*. It is not uncommon for firms to save 1–5 percent of the cost of inventory by using information to understand what they have and how much it costs to make, store, and sell.

A second class of activities and concerns involves conversion of inventory into manufactured goods or sales. Manufacturing often can be automated. Sales are labor intensive. The ability to change supply and demand to meet new circumstances along the supply chain increased enormously in the past 20 years, thanks to more information reporting on events as they occur and better forecasting of demands, supply, and cost. By the early 2000s, enormous improvements had been made. Inventory supplies had declined from 2 months in warehouses in the 1980s to 40 days by the late 1990s to less than 35 days by 2010. Firms accomplished this feat largely by "making to stock" or by buying inventory in a more timely fashion. Quicker turn-arounds from when something is bought to when it is sold translated into growing profits or lower costs of goods and offering prices.

Trends in Supply Chains

The hunt for additional improvements continues. Surveys report four basic requirements for future supply chains which also are emerging as trends now evident in the business world. The first requirement is development of demand-driven supply networks. Data for demand-driven supply networks consists of information that predicts accurately what is needed. It includes how that data is tied to an enterprise's processes to source and allocate people and products in response, from inception to delivery, whether the steps are all in one country or scattered around the world. The second requirement is enhanced visibility, which requires information to extend from providing real-time views of events (currently the more prevalent practice) to visible, open collaboration, which enables people to work together faster and more efficiently. People in a supply chain use and modify (improve) processes and bodies of information that make it easier for them to understand what everyone else in the chain sees and knows. The third requirement, increasingly referred to as sustainability, entails using information to understand cost versus efficiency through balancing a mix of costs and sources of services while maintaining both the economic welfare of the firm and the natural environment. The fourth requirement is managing risks of failure or damage caused by an unanticipated event, such as a natural disaster. This entails using information to establish policies and programs that protect the firm and its supply chains.

Above these four activities as an overarching activity is the pervasive expansion in collaborative planning, forecasting, and replenishment of goods and services through formal processes that are documented and richly endowed with information shared with all involved parties. Surveys of supply-chain management conducted in the early 2000s report that this trend resulted in improved satisfaction and effectiveness. Forecasting errors as measured by the widely used Mean Absolute Percentage Error (MAPE) method are reported to have declined. This result came about largely as a result of the use of more detailed information and as a result of more participation by players in extended supply chains, such as sales and marketing organizations. Consensus on what to change increased, thereby increasing the coordination of activities and responses to changes documented by informed practices. Managing the flow of activities in a supply chain involves overwhelmingly sharing data and taking actions on the basis of what the data show.

The objectives management aspires to achieve using data from these trends are the same as they have been for decades: to use information to protect an enterprise's ability to make a profit, to contain costs, and to understand what customers want and think. How supply chains are informationalized to continue achieving these goals is still an evolving process.

The most obvious way is in how information is being collected. Until 1980, information entering a supply chain came from the efforts of human clerks. Then, in the 1980s, spreadsheets were used to calculate relationships among data. Also in the 1980s, bar-code scanners began a new trend in collecting information: the use of automation and machine-collected data on the physical movement of goods, including bags of money from one bank to another. Today, the number of machines (largely sensors) that are creating, collecting, and now beginning to analyze data is increasing faster than humans can react to this incoming information in a real-time fashion. Radio-frequency identification tags, which can transmit radio signals to computers, are adding to the information originally provided by bar codes. Meters, actuators, and GPS devices collect information and share it through software to enable tracking of the movement of goods and activities, and to record and report results. Other devices are coordinating their activities more than in previous decades, in effect mimicking some of the collaboration first done by humans in managing and operating supply chains.

A second way supply chains are evolving is through more extended sharing of information. Sharing is taking different forms. Supply chains are becoming oblivious to physical locations. If something is made in China, distributed through the Netherlands, and bought in the United States, the supply chain wraps around the world, with each participant in the chain increasingly aware of progress, bottlenecks, quality, and performance thanks to tailored and *ad hoc* reporting. The trend is one of extreme connectivity and of increasing visibility of the performance of other links to members of the chain (often now referred to as *transparency*).

A third way is through is the use of software to analyze patterns of behavior found in the data collected by sensors and by people who make decisions (corrections) regarding activities (such as movement of inventory), and most importantly to model behavior and possible results of both. An emerging trend involves predicting future behavior of a supply chain, a form of modeling that entails creating and assessing options (models and scenarios) that include rich contextual information, such as marketing demographics, economic data, and the usual product and service information of earlier times. There is growing interest in collecting and analyzing information related to risks and constraints, too. The intent—and ultimately, the result—will be continued shifting of some decision making from humans to information systems as management becomes more confident about the quality of the decision making by software, as it has already done with more mundane activities, such as how much paint a robot in an automotive manufacturing plant should spray on a car.

All this information handling is compounded by ever-growing supply chains—for example, the number of firms that participate in any one company's chain. Between 1995 and 2008 the number of transnational firms—all participants in someone else's supply chains—increased from 38,000 to more than 80,000. Outsourcing of all kinds has been increasing, and it involves diffusion of information along with each activity across multiple countries, time zones, computer systems, social and corporate cultures, regulatory regimes, and societies. In surveys of supply-chain management, from decade to decade, cost containment has remained consistently the number one objective of changing the informational content of supply chains, always surpassing growth in revenues and entering new markets.

Visibility of greatly increasing amounts of information remains problematic, however. An important knowledge-management issue faced by the modern enterprise is how to manage the ever-growing amount of information so as to make it visible to human managers and employees, not simply to software models and sensors that depend on it to trigger automated activities of machines. Some firms want to share information; others do not; others don't believe they should invest additional resources in knowledge management to address this issue.

Tied to the issue of how to manage the ever-growing amount of information is an age-old question: What constitutes the "right" information with which to run an enterprise? This has been a topic of discussion and concern for more than 50 years, because, as a supply chain evolves, so do the types of information needed to manage it. Invariably the problem boils down to organizing work processes so that they become standardized in whatever new circumstances a supply chain must function in. Firms bump up against a lack of useful existing information, or a lack of now-needed new information, and even a lack of tools and technologies with which to collect information efficiently and affordably.

These challenges spill over into smaller supply chains in an enterprise, for example as in human resources. Most firms continue to report that they lack sufficiently qualified leaders and skilled workers to create and informationalize processes to address these shortcomings. All the challenges— acquiring and developing managerial talent, creating learning cultures, developing basic skills, transferring knowledge and experience from more experienced employees to those with less skills, transferring knowledge across enterprises within a value chain—devolve into information.

The Role of Digital Technologies

Nowhere in the modern enterprise have information technologies played a greater role than in support of supply chains. As early as the 1910s, adding machines and calculators were used to track inventory. In the 1920s and the 1930s these were augmented by punched cards. By 1960, the use of computers in inventory management represented one of the most intensive deployments of this technology in the private sector. By the 1960s, it was common for computer salesmen in many companies to joke that the whole computer industry had been cost justified by IT to reduce the cost of their customers' inventories.

But supply chains are not concentrated in a few offices or in a corner of some warehouse. They are physically spread across an entire enterprise, planted in the physical localities of suppliers, distributors, and retail outlets. Therefore, it became necessary to collect information and make it available in highly distributed ways, where people worked, managed, and used data. The history of IT in supply chains is a history of the physical diffusion of technologies in many shapes and sizes to all locations of the modern enterprise. As computers became smaller and less expensive, they spread to more corners of firms. As telecommunications became less expensive and easier to use, as they linked computers together, and as they became capable of moving more and more kinds of information about, data spread to many places.

In time, it became possible to connect many technologies—mainframes, iPods, personal computers, hand-held scanners—into large networks. Today there is no living memory of a time when the modern enterprise was not loaded down with IT supporting supply chains. Today all *Fortune* 1,000 firms and their hundreds of thousands of suppliers and millions of distributors are linked through combinations of corporate-run telecommunications that bind many systems together within an enterprise and extend to the systems of business partners. A parallel network is the Internet, which also enables individual consumers to connect with individuals and departments inside the modern corporation, accessing company websites and portals to view product information, place orders, and communicate with individual employees. With appropriate passwords and security features, intranets—internal versions of the Internet—are used for communications within a company. In use since the late 1990s, these are now a stable part of the modern infrastructure.

In some professions, every employee is connected to the corporate telecommunications network, and, by extension, to its supply chains, and thus is able to receive information relevant to him or her. Miners have laptop computers and cell phones. Eighteen-wheel trucks are virtual data centers, equipped with laptops, sensors, GPS, radio communications, and cell phones. The movements of trucks, trains, and airplanes are automatically monitored by large data centers (often called dispatch centers). When changes in delivery are noted and tracked, they are routinely monitored by customers of FedEx, UPS, and, increasingly, national postal systems. Specialized hand-held devices are used by retail stores to update inventory at the shelf, to place orders with their warehouses or distributors for replenishment, and simultaneously to send warehouse orders to suppliers for more inventory. All the while, data collected for use by the accounting and financial communities in affected firms are delivered to large mainframes, to laptops, and even to smart phones. In short, it is not uncommon for 100 percent of the people involved in a supply chain to use IT routinely every working day in the most advanced economies, or for senior executives to monitor activities even on weekends. Certainly this is done 24 hours a day by employees of participating firms dispersed along a supply chain. Supply chains operate 24 hours a day and 365 days a year, along with their IT.

Information comes in the form of spreadsheets—numbers—but also in the form of graphical representations of activities and presentations. Video cameras track

movements of equipment and goods, and of people providing services. Today, data collected by sensors are added
to numerical or incident files, and software developed in
the early 2000s integrates all these forms of data to almost
recreate events such as the delivery or the theft of goods
in real time. The integrating of information is one of the
newest technological frontiers. Following a long-standing
IT tradition, the ability to do this integration, and subse-
quent modeling and predicting, in a physically dispersed
fashion all over the geographical locations of the enterprise, delivering results across the firm and down to individuals using their preferred IT tools, is increasing. That
is one of the defining characteristics of the modern wired
enterprise.

The Emergence of Service Supply Chains

Another frontier in supply-chain management is the service chain. As employees in the modern enterprise increasingly became providers of services, the hunt for efficiencies
and best practices increased. By about 1990, it was natural
that management would turn to supply-chain-manage-
ment techniques in an attempt to understand services.
The supply-chain method of tracking and the information
needed to support such tracking apply just as well to services, but only now are they being adopted in a disciplined

way. McDonald's and Progressive Insurance are notable exemplars, but they are exceptions; their disciplined approaches are not yet widely practiced.

Subject-area experts and knowledge management perform specific actions. A supply chain might begin with an expert with knowledge in his or her head, and the next link might be the coordinated validation of that expertise by the tasks that person does, influenced, of course, by where they report into within an organization since it is the mission of that person's department or organization that shapes many actions. A third sequential link would be the development of compelling and relevant points of view or use of that expertise, followed by a link showing the activities that individual does in support of other people who want to leverage his or her skills. This service supply chain might be extended with an additional link describing how the enterprise deploys the person's expertise outside the firm, in the form of thought leadership, advertising, and services to its customers. One could draw a series of boxes to depict this simple supply chain moving from left to right.

The information required at each step could be documented, and one could then see the movement of data back and forth, from left to right, and from right to left. Measures of the costs of doing the work of each step could be collected—and they are—along with information on results, such as number and value of problems solved or sales made. Management consulting firms and IT service firms have long used such techniques to give structure to their work and to measure performance. Increasingly, as firms spend more of their time and their assets on services, they are doing the same thing, as was noted in the preceding chapter.

As the amount of information increases, service providers combine their service value chains with more traditional physical supply chains. For example, in recent years there has been increasing demand by buyers to see—gain access to—and to understand their suppliers' supply chains, the suppliers' costs of goods sold, delivery schedules, breakdown of expenses by value chain link, and so forth. Using modeling software, customers can compare prices for the same products from multiple vendors, and all the data can be brought together by means of the Internet for a buyer to examine, or they can allow a software tool to choose from various options on the criterion of least cost, speed of delivery, or availability. Commodity-like services, such as term life or automotive insurance offerings by multiple vendors, also are often compared by means of the Internet.

These trends are causing supply chains to be, as modern managers say, "more visible"—that is, data from one enterprise now are accessible to people and software in another enterprise, as consumers experience when they compare online prices of insurance or automobiles. All major corporations now have documented supply chains, and today their customers and suppliers expect to have access to those supply chains through the use of networked information technologies. Thus, lines are blurring among supply and service chains. Customers see a similar process underway with value chains. Legal boundaries and physical locations of things and people are of less and less importance to the actions taken since value chains transcend legal entities and often mask from the customer the actions of member organizations in these value chains.

Implications

Information in supply chains extends outside the traditional enterprise to suppliers to a firm, to retailers, and often to individual customers. One impetus for this extension is the convenience and the growing ability to send information securely by means of the Internet. The increasing number of participants in an Internet-based supply chain is leading to growing demands for greater visibility across all links in the chain.

Participants are increasingly being compelled to unbundle their value chains, thereby making information about their costs, processes, and performance visible. That trend will make some organizations uncomfortable but is already increasing the amount of information that participants in a supply chain want, indeed need, in order to collaborate more effectively with each other, and that can attract additional sources of business. Examples of the new types of information are online catalogs, project-management reports, performance evaluations, part designs and specifications for suppliers of components, integrated communications tools such as e-mail and online team rooms, change-management communications, best practices, and collaborative tools that include information about specific activities relevant to users. These new bodies of information already enrich the flows of data and knowledge within and across supply chains, helping individuals to work together without necessarily being physically near each other.

A second implication, one not well understood yet, is this: When information about an enterprise and about the work to be done is essentially all the information a worker might see, which organization (department) that information comes from is less relevant than before. Already in the past decade websites have evolved from requiring a user to know in which department or agency information resides to in order to get to it to being able to articulate the kind of information a user wants, regardless of where it resides. That shift, along with clustering of types of information that logically belong together regardless of what department produces it, is happening in supply chains. This trend will continue to erode the "silo-centric" behavior practiced by departments and divisions interested more in their own welfare than in the overall good of the corporation, and the lack of teaming in large corporations, in favor of activities that appear more like an extended enterprise in which the functions in a supply chain are visible to an individual. Behind-the-scenes work still occurs in individual organizations, but increasingly geographic location doesn't matter as much as the data and the work itself. This is an important shift in corporate culture, though it is occurring slowly and almost imperceptibly.

Those charged with managing supply chains, and increasingly their positioning within the Internet, are revisiting old questions about how to use their networks for competitive advantage, to drive down costs, to block competition, to find new customers, to keep existing ones, and to do work well. Some individuals will feel threatened by the possibilities of their supervisors watching their actions more closely than they want than their enterprises by the wide availability of information about their operations accessible by customers and competitors, but the recent history of the modern organization suggests that employees in all parts of an enterprise desire, and will acquire, more and better-managed information.

NEW PRODUCTS AND MARKETING IN A DIGITIZED WORLD

Providing structure and imposing process-management practices upon the work of the enterprise are not limited to the operation of supply chains. Product development, marketing, and customer relations have also been profoundly changed over the past 20 years, thanks to the availability of information far beyond what management had in earlier times. For example, not so long ago products were just objects to be produced and packed with limited documentation for manufacturing workers and customers. Training for employees was largely tacit, and only informal. Only brief instructions (information) were given to customers on how to assemble and use a product. All that has changed, and now even the most mundane products are wrapped in information. This chapter describes the contours of that informationalized part of the present-day enterprise.

The Role of Information in Product Development

Creation and manufacture of products have become infor-mationalized supply chains of their own. Today product developers speak of "inputs," "activities," and "deliver-ables," of "concept phases" and "plan phases," and of for-malized models and plans for "life-cycle phases." These processes have assumed features of a cooking recipe, with information expected to be created and responded to at each phase and with "decision points" injected into the value chain to ensure that people are routinely looking at data to monitor and assess progress through the supply chain from one end to the other, making such decisions as "go," "no go," or "redirect" on the basis of facts, relying on statistical analysis and market information, all before even one widget has been made.

Information about customers' needs and desires are methodically collected, documented, and analyzed before designers determine how the next automobile should look or consulting service for computing should be de-veloped, for example. The concept phase has moved from just someone's bright idea—analogous to "Let's invent the light bulb"—to a methodical approach to existing and needed assets of the enterprise. Such an approach entails assessing what would appeal to customers, analyzing costs and benefits (numerically, of course), and evaluat-ing competitors' capabilities and possible responses. Decisions are now considered "deliverables" accompanied by their underpinning data (not just written or verbalized logic) in support of proposed action. A recent addition to the mix has been the cultivation of insights for use in detailed risk assessments of a new product's potential faults or failures.

Assessments and reliance on increased amounts of information have become essential elements of all product development for several reasons. Increasingly, data make it practicable to attempt to understand "the facts" with which some absolute reality can be documented. We now have a generation of managers, from chief executive officers to newly hired young employees, who have been trained in the formal use of processes and information in the course of their undergraduate and graduate engineering, scientific, or business-school education, and through career-long training in various managerial and operational practices. In addition, the number of individuals who play some role as "input" into the process of product development has increased steadily over the years, and information is needed to coordinate the activities of all these people, some of whom are on a "core team" working on a product, some of whom are peripheral to the company and some of whom (such as advertising experts and product-liability lawyers) are outside the company.

An example of information's expanded presence within the process is the management of life cycles, which are the tasks and decisions used to extend or shorten the development of a product. Major inputs now routinely part of these efforts include project plans, market-opportunity data, and performance data and technical and marketing feedback on new offerings. From that body of information emerge go/no-go decisions, withdrawals from projects, and close-outs of project plans. (Closing an automotive plant, shutting down a laboratory, or laying off hundreds of employees may take months.) Therefore, this phase requires data with which to adjust the size and composition of project teams, additional information with which to manage operational performance of a product or project, additional checklists to ensure that all the steps necessary to end or extend a project are followed, and, in cases of best practices, reviews conducted at the end of a project to uncover lessons learned and these insights, of course, be documented. Even movies are developed this way; for example, fans of movies and television fiction are asked whether the story should end on a happy or a sad note, and then these options are tested on sample audiences.

The Role of Information in Marketing Programs

Concurrent with the imposition of rigorous process-management practices in the development of products and services has been the rise of formalized marketing analysis and programs. These activities are 100 percent about information management. The only time a marketing expert may be involved in the physical aspects of a product might be when he holds up a sample in some conference room or hands it to a photographer to produce an illustration (itself a form of information) for advertising purposes. Marketing has evolved into a formal discipline of its own, consisting of a number of activities, the most important of which involve understanding who the customers are, what they want from a product or a service, what they are willing to pay for it, and how they will use it. Another body of information concerns competitors: who they are, what they offer, how well they are doing (number of units sold by month, quarter, and year), when their next product will be announced, and what new products and services are anticipated. A third cluster of information is environmental: the state of a particular nation's economy, regulatory factors affecting a product's attractiveness and cost (such as the European Union's recycling requirements), and, increasingly in recent years, the carbon footprints of both products and overall corporate activities, such as manufacturing processes.

The variety of information required in marketing activities, not just the volume available or desired, has increased over the years. Regulatory practices, such as the enormously more detailed accounting and financial reporting that the Sarbanes-Oxley Act requires of all American corporations, the EU's requirements for reporting on environmental impacts, and the World Trade Organization's requirements, have driven that trend. But the acceptance of the idea that markets can be studied with the same rigor and scientific (numerical and statistical) discipline as accounting and finance is now universally accepted. Even start-up firms are required to produce formal business plans—including market analyses—with which to persuade venture capitalists to invest in them. The days of a bank or a rich investor agreeing to support a project on the basis of a good story and excellent drawings on the back of a napkin are gone, if they ever existed. Investments (internal or external) routinely run into the tens if not the hundreds of millions of dollars. Today people working on business cases and other analytical projects require financial data; demographic statistics on the number of potential customers; forecasts of sales, revenues, potential costs, and profits; and models of various scenarios and options.

If existing products and services are being enhanced or introduced into new markets, "pipeline reports" are needed. Essentially, a "pipeline report" consists of data on how many units (specific products or services) are on order from various sources, or, for the sale of complex and expensive machinery and consulting services, quantified assessments of how much opportunity exists at each of several steps in a sales cycle (activities routinely engaged in to sell something). These data are numerical, and are often delivered to management as spreadsheets with summary reports either in shorter spreadsheets or as PowerPoint reports with textual assessments of issues, opportunities, and statistical odds of happening. It is not uncommon for large enterprises to have formal review processes, such as monthly or even weekly meetings to review the information and adjust plans and actions.

The same process exists in sales organizations, which also look at similar data although more by specific account, product type, and by territory for existing offerings; marketing teams do the same for potential offerings. At some point in the enterprise, those two data streams are brought together, typically at two levels: the level at which the sales and marketing organizations have to collaborate and the senior leadership level (at which executives have to decide whether to introduce or kill products). These are typically the individuals responsible for sales of existing and anticipated offerings, usually situated at a divisional and group level, and ultimately, corporate.

Because the vast majority of this information is collected and stored in computers, consolidating information and moving it up and down the chain of command and back and forth along a value chain is possible, and so it is done. One can reasonably say that the CEOs of today's *Fortune* 1,000 companies see more data on marketing and sales than their predecessors saw as recently as the 1980s. Spreadsheets were the most widely used business application of personal computers when they came into corporate use in the 1980s, far surpassing word processing and e-mail. Marketing departments used personal computers to gather and organize data relevant to them. Corporations then ported that information to large centralized systems so as to share it more widely across the enterprise. Thus, as in manufacturing and logistical supply chains, information seeped into all corners of a company, regardless of where in the world a firm had physical offices.

The Role of Information in Selling and in Customer-Relations Management

A fundamental trend in the evolution of the modern enterprise has been the expanded reliance on information with which to do sales work. Beginning in the late 1800s or the early 1900s, large corporations began creating best practices and formal processes for tracking customers and conducting sales. Some spectacular achievements in the collection of numerical data about these activities were made as early as the 1920s. Over the next 50 years, reliance on tacit knowledge still predominated in a corporation's use of information. By 2000, however, formal collection of explicit information and disciplined fact-based processes had come into their own in nearly all industries in the most industrialized economies. By the early 2000s, this cluster of activities had acquired its own name: *customer relations management* (CRM). The phrase "supply-chain management" galvanized more structured and informationalized activities in manufacturing and product distribution; "customer relations management" is doing the same for sales.

CRM is not as fully defined as supply-chain management, but its scope has increased rapidly to include such activities as (in the terminology of modern business) customer execution, customer service, retail execution, product category management (marketing), consumer strategic planning, and marketing research, in addition to pipeline reporting in sales. When the important undercurrent of budgetary and forecasting data is added, it is evident that CRM has become an important part of the informational infrastructure of the modern corporation. Most of the innovations began with consumer-products companies, then spread rapidly across all industries. Today the informational requirements center on four activities: executive reporting and brand health analysis, tracking of the performance of new products, advertising and marketing mix spending, and optimization of trade promotion. Sales performance is increasingly being linked or made part of CRM processes and data collection and analysis as well. What data one would collect for each of these activities is obvious enough. Less evident is the current trend of applying an increasing number of analytical tools to understand this ever-growing collection of information and raw numerical data. It is that trend that makes CRM so important to an informationalized enterprise. The methods combine the use of statistical modeling with nearly real-time availability of data and information. There is an increasing need for speed of analysis, so as to identify trends sooner than competitors also using such techniques, to change prices, or to introduce new products to the market at the right times. Recent price wars between Amazon and Barnes and Noble over e-book readers, between iTunes and traditional music publishers over music, and between the iPhone and other smart phones and their allied network providers that occurred over hours and days instead of over weeks and months, became possible in shorter periods of time largely because of rapid access to timely information. The alternative was to respond to competition without knowing the potential effects of, for example, lowering the price of a product a few hours after a competitor did so. Speed is, thus, an important priority in assessing the value and use of information, a topic to which I will come back a number of times.

Marketing and sales consume an enormous amount of time at all levels of an enterprise, because they can rapidly spiral out of control. Yet marketing and sales also have historically been a rich area of cost cutting, and hence for improving profits. How successful a firm is with one form of distribution—direct sales force vs. working through retailers or wholesales, for example—becomes increasingly important and is always linked directly to the firm's advertising strategies. The manufacturers of some consumer products spend as much as a third of their cost for an offering just on advertising.

Corporations are building informational infrastructures in support of CRM. This started with supply-chain management in the 1970s and the 1980s. Just as speed of collection, analysis, and availability are essential, so too is the *integration* of diverse sets of data and information. That second feature is increasingly required because of the variety of data that must be pulled together in order to make fact-based decisions. As a result, much attention is paid to data management, to the creation of analytical infrastructures (both software and processes), and to applying best practices of knowledge management not only regarding CRM but across many processes in an enterprise, although more typically still within the confines of individual divisions within a company. These practices are emerging in the automated integration of data drawn from internal and external sources, from people, and from sensors. Embedding metrics and other analytical tools into work with customers as it occurs is increasingly evident in the modern enterprise. The creation of tools and reports that pop out findings either at pre-scheduled times (such as in a weekly sales cadence review) or as *ad hoc* notifications that something has just changed (e.g., that sales of a particular product increased or decreased beyond normal, pre-determined ranges of performance) are also coming into wide use.

Consumer goods companies in particular, but all corporations in general, face information-related stumbling blocks that involve data and knowledge. In the case of information itself, inconsistent formats for data make it difficult to combine reports; this probably is the oldest and most familiar issue. In addition, access to the right information is limited, if any information is available at all, and the integration of software and operational infrastructures for sharing information is inadequate. Such problems are chronic throughout the modern enterprise, but nowhere more so than in the newest areas of data collection and analysis, such as CRM. Yet, since all information is not created by one enterprise (rather, information is created by many yet accessible across a firm), keeping up with the expanding volume of data also available to competitors is now a serious managerial problem. Growing volumes of data make all these issues more like challenges than topics of interest, and more intense and of greater concern.

The oldest body of information that illustrates the problem consists of retail point-of-sale (POS) data. POS cash registers attached to in-store computers that in turn were connected to warehouses and to divisions of the parent corporation began collecting orders of magnitude volumes of data on individual transactions in the late 1970s.

For example, by the late 1980s Wal-Mart could learn exactly how many particular items were sold on any particular day by store, by region, by country, by product group, and, in some instances, by type of customer. By the early 1980s, some retailers were gathering more pieces of information in one day than the rest of their enterprise collected as a whole in a year. We now face a similar increase in data as a result of the use of sensors, such as those provided by RFID tags and GPS monitoring. As with POS data, the hunt for a way to integrate new bodies of information is a major activity of the modern enterprise.

Historically, CRM's information evolution paralleled those of other groups of informed activities within an enterprise. First, management wanted to know sales volumes and compared to those of their competitors. That requirement remains. Then came analysis of the best-performing and worst-performing products, stores, weeks, quarters, clusters, and territories. Software generated lists that ranked performance—for example, by products and territories, by which sales representatives were ahead of their sales goals for the year to date or the current month, or behind them, by a certain percentage. Marketing and sales "what if" became the next layer of information, generating answers to such questions as "What price point will drive optimal sales?" and "What is the optimal assortment of goods in a store?" Simultaneously, information gathering and analysis occurred in real time, but also analyses in shorter periods of time, evolving quickly from quarterly to weekly, and now routinely daily or hourly (the latter in particular by retail firms).

The current frontier of information management is the move toward more structured predictions of coming events and possibilities. Much has been written about this, and a great deal has been done. But it remains a frontier because of the recent arrival of a new generation of software tools and methods that are yet to be fully applied by CRM and sales management. But sales and marketing managers know what they want to know: What new products will be successful in the market next year? What promotional activities will increase sales over the summer? The latter often is one of the most asked questions in consumer electronics firms regarding the Christmas sales season and the equally challenging first quarter of every year.

Surveys of CRM and sales operations suggest, however, that much work remains to be done to integrate existing sets of data. Everyone wants a forecast—predictions. And predictions become more accurate as the data injected into the process increase in volume and quality, as is also true of weather prediction. Fifty years ago, a weather forecast was at best good locally for the next two or perhaps three days. Now we routinely and accurately learn about the weather for the next ten days, and national weather forecasters offer general predictions of trends for the hurricane season, the winter, and the next summer. All these changes were made possible by the collection of huge quantities of data, the integration of those data, and improved modeling. That is where the modern enterprise is headed, but it has a ways to go to catch up with the weather forecasters.

What is it about information that worries CRM executives? Surveys conducted in 2008–2010 suggest some answers. They know that the quantity of data created in a year now exceeds the quantity of data created in the previous 5,000 years, and that the world now has nearly 5 billion cell phones in use and about 3 billion Internet users. For these executives, the challenge is to keep up with these data-generating tools but also to answer such basic questions as "How do I use all the data?" and "What does _____ mean for my business?" They complain that using exponentially growing volumes of data is difficult, requiring data management far beyond what IT technicians were capable of even as recently as the 1990s. Closing the gap between insight and action is the main managerial challenge they report facing, despite the fact that they collect more information about more things at every step of every CRM transaction and every sales process.

Customers have been busy too, using information to such an extent that in some industries the informational balance of power has shifted toward them, nearly enabling them to dictate the enterprise's priorities. Thanks to the fact that more than a billion users of the Internet now routinely access information online, surveys show that just over 50 percent of consumers report using it to compare features and prices of products—about 25 percent while in a store, using a mobile telephone. About 10 percent even send text messages to friends and family members while in a store to ask for advice on what to buy. While CRM and marketing departments try to understand consumers by tracking what they use the Internet for, customers are collaborating in user groups, posting quality rankings of products on websites, and disseminating opinions, facts, and findings about products electronically. Favorable reports from this community lead to more sales; unfavorable ones are hard to overcome. As always, customers trust each other more than they trust vendors to report the "facts."

Survey feedback also suggests that those most able to deal with the gap between what customers know and report and what companies learn through traditional marketing and sales reporting have skills that are essential in an organization held together by data and information. They focus on integrating data collection and insight into processes, using traditional best practices and new sources of data (e.g., demographic, credit reports, GPS and RFID devices). They recruit and nurture individuals capable of doing knowledge-management work, with an emphasis on managing the intake, the care, and the flow of data and information. (This is not usually an IT job, but it can be; it requires uncovering insights needed to make managerial decisions of a non-IT nature.) They align data collection and data analysis with the most obvious managerial best practices. For example, they begin by collecting information about customers, not about products; information about products comes next in priority. Knowing well the environment in which they have to work comes first, because a person with such knowledge can use experience and best practices to develop and execute plans so as to achieve positive financial results. Contacts with customers ("moments of truth") are documented and analyzed. Novel insights occur. For example, we now know that customers who are well informed about a firm and its products and services tend to be more loyal, coming back to that firm for more products. (Apple has become a familiar example of that phenomenon.) Data from surveys suggest that customers are four times as likely to buy a firm's products if the vendor fixes problems their customers tell them exist with existing offerings. To do that requires understanding in considerable detail, and in different forms, what customers are thinking. Hence, we have a clear reason for why the processes described in this chapter exist and are becoming more informationalized.

Yet sales and marketing professionals have a ways to go to satisfy themselves. Today's CRM managers have been surrounded by a great deal of data, information, and computers throughout their careers. Only about 20 percent of them feel that they have the tools they need to do what is described in this chapter, yet their fathers would have been amazed at how much information they have today. In surveys, the majority of CRM managers report that success comes when they have better-managed data, and they are prepared to invest in IT tools and in new sources of information. Sales organizations seem to be the best equipped, marketing organizations the most poorly served. This is not surprising: most sales information consists of explicit data, whereas marketing requires contextual tactical information, which is much harder to collect, integrate, and assess.

Informationalizing Customers

Corporations have long understood that informed customers buy more goods and services from them. For decades the definition of an informed customer was simply "an individual who is familiar with the features of a product and with what it costs relative to other products, and who knows how to use it correctly." The more complex a product, the more "education" and "training" a vendor had to provide to customers. The more competitive the market, the more important advertising was. A recent trend in advertising has been the addition of more facts about a product, such as survey and study results that demonstrate a product's superiority over another, as one sees, for example in the United States, with advertisements for automobiles touting results that announce proudly their product's reliability and advertisements for pharmaceuticals touting results that their medication's effectiveness. As corporations shifted responsibility for assembling and maintaining products to consumers (beginning after World War II), the amount of instructions required by consumers to accomplish those tasks increased. By the time personal computers, other digital consumer goods, and other complex products became available to consumers, lengthy manuals quickly became essential. Now manuals usually are available both on paper and online.

By the early 2000s, the amount of information presented to customers, indeed required by them, had increased in many industries to such an extent that providing large amounts of information now is the norm in product packaging. Today a company's website usually offers, in addition to more typical information about a product's features, instructions in many languages on assembling and using the product and on how to diagnose problems and make simple repairs. In addition, corporations are offering "chat rooms" in which users can share information about their use of a product, links to other websites that give information about the context in which a product is used, news reports about the firm and its offerings, and (of course) advertisements. Companies are also providing access to reports relevant to their goods and services, such as scientific papers related to medical products.

Information aggregators began appearing on the Internet in the 1990s. Information aggregators are organizations that scan online catalogs and corporate databases for information that enables consumers to compare the features, costs, and customer ratings on quality and performance of many products from many vendors. This expands on the original idea of the magazine *Consumer Reports*, covering many kinds of consumer and industrial products available from sources all around the world. Corporations are building communities of practice (and communities of shared interest) within consumer communities centered on a brand (such as Apple) or a product (such as a specific model of automobile). This development has proved highly popular.

Another development involves enhancing a product with ancillary offerings. Take, for example, the humble book, which used to be a single product (or perhaps two or more if a book had been translated). Today, in addition to the book *per se* there are CD versions, electronic editions, summary podcasts, individual chapters for sale in both hardbound and softbound copies, authors' websites, chat rooms (sponsored by various organizations or by a book's publisher), an author's home page on the Internet, and tailored publishing (in which chapters from multiple books are integrated into new books). Authors write short summaries of their books and of chapters in them, which are immediately made available to potential customers as advertisements, as free content, or for sale. Video media are increasingly becoming elements of the informationalized package in which a book is ensconced. DVDs of movies and television programs include additional material, such as unpublished scenes and interviews with directors and actors.

Implications

This chapter has discussed the processes and flows of information in a corporation that are most visible to employees, customers, government officials, competitors, the press, and the public. Tied to these processes and flows of information is the "nuts-and-bolts" work done by employees to create images of the firm. These are also some of the most diverse, complex, and expanding bodies of data and insights pouring into and out of a corporation. They make it seem relatively insular and simple to collect and use accounting information, financial information, manufacturing information, and other traditional information, if only because most of those older bodies of data are largely numerical and lend themselves relatively easily to automation and modeling. Another feature of the newer types of information described in this chapter is that they are the ones most discussed in conversations about social networking, use of the Internet, security of data, privacy of information, advertising, product recalls, quality rankings, and regulatory considerations. Finally, these are the most rapidly growing bodies of data. Data pour into the modern corporation from sensors and from multiple websites. A corporation cannot shape or control this information; it can only use it; and it must integrate the information in order to make sense of it.

Mixtures of data, information, insights, and wisdom about customers, products, markets and how a firm deals with each of these aspects of their business run the gamut from explicit to tacit knowledge. They change rapidly, and they are having profound effects on the daily work of the enterprise. For example, the real-time images coming from BP's oil spill in the Gulf of Mexico in 2010 affected the company's image, its relations with peer firms, its interactions with both the U.S. and British governments, and the value of its stock. Conversely, at the same time, positive images and data related to sales and demand made Apple a darling of Wall Street and one of the most admired firms in the world.

In the years to come, firms will spend more time learning how to collect, manage, and use information than they will spend on any other collections of data they currently use comfortably.

The challenges for management will depend on the degree to which their companies can integrate internal and

A corporation cannot shape or control this information; it can only use it; and it must integrate the information in order to make sense of it.

external data in one location or a few locations (virtual and real), the extent to which customers can share and borrow data with which to influence their relations with a company and affect and inform their own buying habits, and how management and expert employees can enrich data for analysis. Companies will have to extend their automated collection and analysis of disparate data in order to convert them into actionable insights available in a timely manner. The managements of many corporations already are asking how well they are developing useful insights into customers' shopping behaviors. In addition, they are asking "To what extent are we pushing those insights back into other processes in the firm, such as those that shape the fundamental business strategies of the firm or to the work of supply chains?"

Because so many of these questions are influenced by the technologies underpinning the collection, storage, analysis, flow, and use of information, the next chapter is devoted to that "technological plumbing." This is an urgent topic because the technology is still changing as quickly as it has in each decade since World War II. We have only to think about the recent injection into the economy of social networks and smart phones—neither of which was of concern to the modern enterprise as recently as 2000—to know that IT is still evolving, emerging, and innovating.

"DIGITAL PLUMBING" IN THE MODERN ORGANIZATION

All enterprises, regardless of size, have a great deal of computing and communications hardware and software installed. Their employees do, too. There is an inaccurate view which holds that the clutter of technologies is just that—a disorganized hodgepodge of gadgets, desk drawers full of old cell phones and calculators whose batteries died a long time ago, and storerooms full of ancient PCs that someone intends to recycle someday. To be sure, there are multiple generations of equipment and software in use, and there are systems that do not make it easy to move data from one piece of equipment to another, but underneath it all, and behind the scenes, something quite different has been emerging as the "digital plumbing" of the modern organization, in both the public and the private sector, with virtually no exceptions.

The annual expenditure of nearly $4 trillion on information technology, of which about half goes explicitly into the digital infrastructures of organizations, has resulted in some common patterns of deployment. These can lead us to see the networked workplace in new ways. Perhaps most important, IT infrastructures collect and make available an enormous amount of useful information. It is no accident that individuals and organizations have spent tens of trillions of dollars on information and communication technology (ICT) in the past 50 years, or that expenditures on ICT today consume 6–7 percent of the world's total GDP.

Information Networks for Systems of Systems

In the 1970s, as people started using personal computers, terminals, and big computers in combination to share information, corporate managements began implementing an extended three-prong process. First, they rationalized the use of technology to gain control over expenditures of all types on ICT. Second, they took steps to make the flow of digitized data around the enterprise, the government agency, and (later) the university increasingly effective and ubiquitous. Third, and most recently, a primary objective has been to protect data contained in these systems. By 1980, the humble data-processing manager had been elevated to divisional vice president of Management Information Systems (MIS). By 1990, that individual was an executive—perhaps the corporation's Chief Information Officer (CIO). The first two classes of management protected networks and data within their divisions. CIOs acquired a mandate almost as broad as that of the Chief Financial Officer (CFO). Beyond their responsibilities for acquiring, protecting, and using hardware and software, CIOs were now responsible for helping all employees use technology in support of their activities as knowledge workers. Information was as valuable as money and inventory, and loss of information was as devastating as usurpation of a patent or industrial espionage. By the early 2000s, IT organizations had gone from consuming 1–1.7 percent of a corporation's budget to an average closer to 5–9 percent, varying by industry.

We are now at a point where digital infrastructures can be seen as systems of systems—ecosystems made up of processes, not only of hardware and software. An enterprise is made up of collections of processes, and so are the data that each process requires and is a part of—data which are attached to work flows with ICT. A city consists of a system of systems. Systems supporting health, fire protection, policing, traffic management, provision of clean water, waste management, and economic development must be coordinated, managed, and continuously improved, or at least maintained, in order for the community to work. Mayors view their management process and the work of their employees as fitting into such systems. Similarly, the modern corporation thinks of its information and technologies

We are now at a point where digital infra-structures can be seen as systems of systems—ecosystems made up of processes, not only of hardware and software.

of all kinds as elements in a collection of tools that must be coordinated and must be effective in order for the firm to do its work. Projects have to be cost justified, technical standards have to be imposed on everyone, and data-security and privacy practices have to be established and maintained. Those activities are many of the fundamental tasks of the modern CIO. There is an increasing impetus to assert leadership in suggesting to users of these technologies how best to leverage ICT for the betterment of the firm. Corporate-wide strategies, identification of new sales opportunities, organizations and tasks that are candidates for cost containment, and employee development, among other tasks, are now included in a CIO's itinerary.

Fundamental components of the system of systems mirror those described earlier for supply chains: multiple networks (private, intranet, Internet) across which data come into and go out of the enterprise and through different networks, and the various places in which data are stored (ranging from a smart phone to a large database connected to a supercomputer in a secure and air-conditioned "glass house" data center). Recently these data (often called multimedia) have included video, spreadsheets, short e-mails, 100-page PowerPoint decks, and book-length PDF files. "Islands of automation" was once a term used to describe pockets of digitized information and the computing done with such data; today those pockets have been linked so closely together that instead one can think more in terms of *continents* of automation.

A fundamental feature of IT, and a general IT practice that always existed in one form or another, is decentralized decision making about when various pieces of the "systems of systems" of ICT should be replaced. In one part of the enterprise, an employee's aging Dell laptop computer would be replaced with a shiny new Apple. Elsewhere in the enterprise, an old edition of a database-management software tool would be replaced with another, with no consideration given as to whether the mainframe system was able to recognize and read the data in the aforementioned employee's Apple laptop. In such decisions and isolated actions—taken every day in a typical mid-size to large enterprise, and often several times a year by individuals at home—we can see an almost biological process at work. To get an idea of what is happening digitally in the modern enterprise, think of the various pieces of hardware and software as cells in a living being, many of which are replaced every day. The same applies to information. Old data are continuously replaced with new data, in some instances updating other files and in many occasions not. Information moves from one part of a firm to another part in new directions, not just over the well-worn paths of existing processes and practices. That is the reality with which technological "systems of systems" management deals today.

Most of the ongoing changes are made by humans, but an increasing percentage of them are made and implemented by software. As sensors send in data, information about inventory levels, temperatures, the speeds of trucks, and traffic congestion in a city is collected and, increasingly, interconnected. Software also does the same thing to IT itself. Since the 1970s, vendors have installed software on mainframes to track technical "hiccups" and to silently repair problems while humans sleep. Security patches delivered by Microsoft to a corporate user's laptop computer are installed automatically while the user types away. In short, machines (not always computers), software, and people are continuously changing the elements of information, their underlying technologies and, as a result, the work, processes, and role of the modern enterprise. This is not Big Brother at work; it is a continuously dynamic process in which human activities (analogous to the growth and decay of cells) is going on in tandem with digital tools everywhere in the modern enterprise.

Another feature of the modern system of systems is a form of connectivity widely known as *convergence*, which involves linking technologies and information together. It happens so silently and incrementally that it is almost imperceptible. For examples, messages left on a person's telephone are now routinely also posted to his or her computer, and can be listened to even while the person is doing other work with the machine. "Webinars" include presentations on a large flat-panel screen hanging on a wall fed with images off the Internet, music, lectures, and verbal reports delivered through a laptop, and the simultaneous ability to send text messages to other participants in a digitized meeting. Such meetings routinely involve text, broadcasting, telephony, texting, and PowerPoint presentations. The costs of doing these things have fallen so much that simple versions of convergence are widely available, some for free. (Millions of families use Skype to hold video-and-telephone conversations with relatives in real time.)

Communications and digital technologies have made possible three styles of work that now have been adopted widely. First, employees in a department can work together relatively interactively while living in various parts of the world, with little or no travel required. They can see each other online, and communicate in real time, at all hours of the day. Large enterprises, therefore, increasingly align employees from around the world by skills, in order to create synergies and efficiencies. Second, reliance on larger bodies of information has led to a series of social and business practices made possible by such technologies as software to manage massive sets of data and others that perform analytical functions on collections of digitized information. These practices include extensive use of PowerPoint presentations, spreadsheets, and shared team rooms in the course of normal organizational meetings. Because these behaviors transcend enterprises, customers and suppliers, all expect the same kind of information for such inter-organizational meetings presented in familiar forms. Third, people have to take the effects of working across time zones into account more than ever before, since participants in a meeting can easily be many time zones apart. Only a generation ago, such gatherings were science fiction. Now, there is much debate about how important physical meetings really are.

Where Information Is Housed and Hidden

IT experts used to think of data and information as stored in computers. Knowledge-management gurus more often thought of documents and people's brains as where information resided. Network administrators remind us of how many exabytes of data are in transit over a network, or making their way through the Internet, at any moment. Librarians and book collectors think in terms of paper and buildings filled with the ephemera of human knowledge. Biologists talk about instinct or genetic coding that contain instructions and information stored in DNA, while other scientists speak about the genius of ants and the wisdom of crowds. Where is information housed in the modern enterprise?

The answer is that it is lodged in many places, obviously, but more interestingly in many ways. Employees in modern enterprises routinely think of data and information as stored in computers, and as available by means of the Internet. To be sure, a great deal of information is stored in computers and can be accessed and used online. And the amount of data stored in electronic forms continues to double in ever-shorter periods of time. A majority of IT experts expect that the volume of information and the variety of formats and forms in which it is stored will continue to grow rapidly. The diffusion of places within an enterprise and its broader social and operational ecosystem of mobile employees working inside and outside the physical and legal boundaries of the enterprise has been increasing sharply too since the mid 1990s. The numbers and types of other participants sharing and using data, such as customers and suppliers, are increasing too. As machines acquire more intelligence (that is, embedded computing with which to do such things as adjust their own performance), they too will become major repositories of data that humans will want to access and protect.

Other places where information resides aren't always acknowledged. Studies of researchers in computer science, for example, clearly show that they use paper formats (printouts, journals, and books) as well as digital ones. Walk into a book editor's office and you will see piles of paper manuscripts, even though much editorial work now is done electronically. Often an accountant's workspace is piled high with printouts of spreadsheets. Legal departments are full of paper, despite the fact that lawyers are extensive users of online databases. To be sure, much information that once would have been on paper is now in electronic form, but there are three reasons why paper documents will not disappear:

- legal requirements in some countries that call for hard copies of contracts and other documents

- old habits and old policies on retention of corporate records, even in some of the world's most high-tech firms

- human thinking practices.

Human thinking practices are increasingly being examined by experts on how people work and on how the brain operates, and by students of social conditioning and culture. People often need to look at data in a physical way, such as on paper, 3×5 cards, a stack of paper receipts, even a box of objects rather than just as information on a flat screen. For example, when one is reading a 300-page book and has completed reading the first 100 pages, one has a stronger sense of how much remains to be read than if one is reading the same text on an electronic device that indicates there are 200 pages yet to consume only in a non-physical way. The physically sensed 200 pages register more vibrantly in the brain than the abstract notion of 200 pages. The latter is an intellectual activity requiring use of a portion of the brain that is still evolving. The desire for physicality goes a long way toward explaining why computer scientists at Xerox PARC, at IBM's Watson Research Laboratory, and at Microsoft use a combination of paper, CDs, laptop computers, and huge databases to do their work.

As the modern enterprise relies more and more on digitized information, it remains deeply rooted in earlier human practices for the collection and use of data, including books and printouts of computer files. Paper still has to be acknowledged as a major repository of an enterprise's information. Paper documents still can be found in employees' briefcases, in the trunks of their cars, in their home offices or basements, and in customers' offices.

Thus, the old problems concerning physical lockup of files in an office remain; indeed, they are exacerbated by the number of places outside the modern enterprise where employees take their data. So too is the problem of creating, maintaining and keeping current backup copies. Now that eliminating the use of paper is a widespread goal, how many paper documents are backed up with duplicate printed copies? Shredding paper documents is fine as long as soft copies of their contents are stored safely for future use; otherwise, it remains a questionable practice.

In addition to information housed in computers and in paper, there is information housed in the human brain (already discussed in the context of knowledge management). For years KM experts have recognized that the three places in which information resides—computers, papers, and brains—should be coordinated, and that the combined information should be leveraged as a tool for gaining competitive advantage or for improving the efficiency of an enterprise. This is why many corporations (especially *Fortune* 1,000 companies and other large enterprises) have established "centers of competence" (also known as "centers of excellence") to facilitate the use of information and to optimize the cost of doing knowledge work.

Because paper media, portable digital media, and human brains will continue to co-exist for years to come, the question as to where this precious corporate asset—information—is housed, used, and protected will remain difficult to answer. In any case, the importance of knowing where information is housed and managed will increase.

The Evolution of Information Technology

Knowing how information technologies permeate an organization is important, since they can help optimize the availability and use of data or can just as easily constrain it. There is a vast literature on the subject of IT. Corporations have been using computers since the start of the 1950s, leaving behind a large body of history of their experiences with the technology. From this record we can distil several patterns of adoption that are nearly universal and that transcend both time and type of technology.

First, the cost of doing a transaction on a computer (e.g., adding a piece of information or calculating an answer) generally falls by 20–40 percent each year. Of course, more computing is required as activities become more complex, so a firm may not experience these declines in transaction costs. As computing declines in cost, demand for its use increases. Flat-screen televisions cost about $5,000 when they first appeared in the market; today one can be had for $600. A homeowner might have purchased only one flat-screen TV for $5,000, but today a home may contain several of them, acquired at various prices as their cost fell. The household's total expenditures on TV sets may be about $3,000 or $4,000. The flat-screen TVs probably were purchased before replacements for old tube TVs were needed because their new functions were attractive. The same phenomenon is at work in corporations.

Second, the proportion of expenditures that goes to software and IT services increases incrementally as the expense of computer hardware falls. In the 1960s, more than 80 percent of expenditures on IT were for digital machines; today the same percentage pays for software, maintenance, and consulting. Services rise in cost faster than software, while the cost of hardware continues to decline. One can expect this pattern to continue for the foreseeable future, particularly as data centers and their hardware are consolidated through outsourcing, cloud computing, and use of the Internet for a company's backbone communications infrastructure.

Third, various computer systems of different ages and degrees of incompatibility always exist concurrently, which means that some digitized data residing in a computer can't easily be shared with other parts of the enterprise. To be sure, much progress has been made since the late 1960s to address this problem; however, one can reasonably assume it will never be fully resolved, since new systems that may not be compatible with previous ones keep on appearing. As a rule of thumb, however, a new version of a software package will normally be able to read data stored in some earlier edition of the programs (a function known as *backward compatibility*). People making decisions to acquire hardware and software must and usually do consider compatibility, asking "Will my existing data be accessible through the new IT?" If the answer is "No," or "Maybe not," or "I don't know," tests must be conducted. If changes to the technology will be necessary, they can be planned for before the change to the new IT is made.

Fourth, end users generally do not pay as much attention to the implications of corporate technical standards as technical staffs do. Yet adherence to standards makes the flow of information through an enterprise easier to accomplish; it also can reduce the cost of information, IT hardware and software, and their use by people across the entire enterprise. This is why CIOs favor enforcement of technical standards. End users will frequently acquire a system that meets as close as possible their own information usage requirements with less consideration for corporate standards unless mandated to do so, and even then may not. For example, an engineer might acquire a software tool to manage how data is stored and moved about which works within her own computer but when she attempts to send that data to another department, it cannot be read over there because the software tool used originally is incompatible with the receiving computer. IT organizations try to accommodate the arrival of technologies that may not be compatible with other installed systems in order to please their stakeholders. This is a problem for both the users and the IT organization, and each group should establish practices that minimize technical tensions resulting from deviations from standards. When IT organizations and users collaborate in setting and changing technical standards, access to information generally improves and overall costs for IT and managing or using information stabilize or even declines. The most data-intensive businesses—including Wal-Mart, Google, Citibank, IBM, and Amazon—address technical standards and practices at levels as high as the CEO and presidential levels.

Fifth, installing major systems and bringing them into operation takes 50–200 percent longer than was planned.

However, they remain in use 50–200 percent longer than was planned. This is attributable to over-optimistic planning, to unanticipated problems at the start of a project, and to the life cycle of an IT use, yet it is also a result of expense and complexity of replacing these with something new. Incremental change is the widely deployed strategy embraced by IT organizations and end users. For users of information, life changes incrementally, often imperceptibly, in ways that aren't appreciated until about 10 years later, when they look back and see that the types of information they use, the way they do their work, and how the enterprise is organized and functions have changed. They tell newspaper reporters that they "made a revolution," and books are published about them, but historians discover that in reality these users "made an evolution." The same occurred with their IT infrastructure, with the similar rates of change.

The pervasive pattern of informationalized behavior is one of grafting different data files onto existing digitized records, such as adding video to text files, or making spreadsheets directly accessible from a PowerPoint presentation, or, for that matter, video too in that same presentation deck. People who rely extensively on information want to add to what they have, much like a scholar who would rather add newly published books to her library than replace old books with new copies of the same books.

The one notorious exception—and it occurs widely in corporations—is the deletion of earlier versions of presentations, old e-mail, and statistical data on past activities that law doesn't require a corporation to preserve. Though almost universally ignored, this topic is worthy of corporate consideration, since information is an asset. Too often, old files are discarded, almost as if you were to throw away coins minted two years ago because the exchange rate for your country's currency had declined. Two-year-old coins still have value, and so do many types of old information. Eventually corporations will recognize that fact, but in the meantime IT departments chastise users for filling up their laptops' inexpensive hard drives, and departments continue to have contests to see who can throw out the most material when they move from one building to another.

Implications

Patterns of use, trends in adoption of IT, and general ways of using IT apply closely to information practices and equipment. A paper-making machine that costs tens of millions of dollars has built-in computers, and the arrival, the use, and the replacement of such a machine often follows the same path as the arrival, use, and replacement of Internet-based software and data or a million-dollar computer.

Users of information have personal and departmental work habits that change slower than one might expect or want. These patterns of behavior are so subliminal that they are recognized only by academic sociologists or by knowledge-management experts hidden away deep in tiny corners in their enterprises. Neither KM experts nor sociologists have much influence in setting corporate strategy regarding implementation of practices to optimize use of information in the firm.

The one obvious exception, of course, is the IT function, which collectively sets policies and make visible practices involved in the use of computing and communications technologies, therefore by default, digitized information. Information technologies are so visible and obvious that the purpose of the first paragraph of this book, and the whole purpose of this volume, was to get past this visible feature of the modern enterprise so as to understand the fundamental justification for the use of IT: information.

There is an old dream, dating back many hundreds of years and revived frequently in the past 50 years: the creation of an organization-wide giant brain, a single repository where all information inside an enterprise would be in one place, so everyone could have access to it and could use it effectively and easily. The artificial-intelligence community spoke of this in the 1950s, developers of databases spoke of it in the 1960s and the 1970s, and more recently it became the stated objective of Google and Wikipedia.

Great progress has been made toward that end, but the amount of information that resides in one place still remains a tiny fraction of what an organization has within its walls (and also physically outside of it) and between the ears of its employees, its former employees, its customers, its competitors, its enemies, and the outside world in general. But (to paraphrase a distinguished politician) the dream lives, and the fight goes on. As technology improves and becomes capable of handling ever-larger amounts of information of various kinds, the dream will seem ever more possible. In the interim, enterprises continue to change, thanks to their growing use of information and also to the use of information by the world at large.

THE STRUCTURE OF
THE MODERN ORGANIZATION

This chapter is about how the resources of the modern organization are organized. The word "organization" is used here because many of the trends described here are occurring in universities and in government agencies, not just in business enterprises. These trends are evident all over the world, even in places one would think have yet to embrace the Information Age. All major surveys of modern societies, governments, and businesses have essentially concluded that more than 90 percent of the world is embracing the Information Age in some form. The current worldwide movement of more than a billion people out of poverty and into the middle class is simply the most current and visible testimony to that reality. This chapter follows a long-standing managerial practice that form follows function—that is, that enterprises organize in ways that are useful in the performance of their work, most notably the ways discussed in earlier chapters.

The modern enterprise has been undergoing significant changes in the past 30 years, and it is just now entering a new phase of evolution that can best be summarized with the biological metaphor of an ecosystem of systems comprising partners, firms, and supply chains. These partners, firms, and supply chains are loosely dispersed, constantly changing in form, driven by the power of well-used information, and assisted in their work by ubiquitous use of information technologies. It is a richly diverse environment, with thousands of types of "ants," "birds," and "large mammals" all evolving into tall and short, fat and thin, big and strong, smart and less smart creatures of capitalism. The driving force behind all these changes, as in biology, is a combination of things others are doing (which require responses) and the increasing sophistication of the role of information, which also is evolving. As is suggested throughout this book, the corporate enterprise, if viewed as a species, would have to be described as currently in a state of rapid evolution, a phenomenon that, as biologists have long recognized, also occurs with living creatures, which go through periods of more extensive rapid evolution or after episodes of change begin in their environment.

Business models and organizational structures are by-products of how enterprises want to sell their goods and services, of the economics of those offerings, of the nature of their competition, of the effects of regulations and environmental conditions, of the attitudes and expectations

The modern enterprise has been undergoing significant changes in the past 30 years, and it is just now entering a new phase of evolution that can best be summarized with the biological metaphor of an ecosystem of systems comprising partners, firms, and supply chains.

of their customers, and of the corporation's culture (most specifically, how employees are rewarded and punished). Incentives within an enterprise and corporate culture, particularly the nature of the incentives (read measurements of performance) of an employee, are too often dismissed as less important. Yet all these various environmental realities play profound roles in how enterprises are organized and how they operate. As was demonstrated in earlier chapters, each of this realities is supported by information to some degree, most recently by more information rather than less. Business models, therefore, have a profound influence on the kind of information that is gathered and used, on its organization, and on its effectiveness. Surveys of information handling over the past 10 years showed that firms (not just individual users within them) attempt overtly to leverage information to outperform those that don't do so.

The Old Way: Hierarchy and Control

Between the 1870s and the mid 1990s, managements organized information in a way that reflected the way companies and corporations were structured in that long period. By 1940, with the concept of the division well established in the largest enterprises, one could see information organized (that is to say housed) within a department or a division. It was created for and used by individuals within the department or division, with little sharing outside the walls of those organizational structures. This was true of paper files and, increasingly, of digital records, first in computers that could not transmit data to other systems, and later in systems within a department or a division. In the 1970s, the 1980s, and the 1990s, as organizations increasingly distributed work, thus flattening their hierarchies, information also spread about the enterprise, sometimes crossing divisions, and increasingly spilling out to other firms in one's supply chains. (This was made possible largely by IT's ability to move information into various parts of an organization using computers of different sizes that matched what a department or some other institution could afford or what it needed.)

Through the twentieth century, as the volume of information on which people became dependent increased, the management and control of data became more centralized within departments and divisions, as did corporate-wide practices and rules for managing access to and preservation of these data. Access remained largely "siloed" within divisions until the 1980s. As information-handling technologies evolved, these too were used to reinforce the more consolidated practices, with large centralized data centers the epitome of the modern corporation as early as the 1950s. That trend did not begin to change substantively until the late 1980s, when "distributive processing" became more the norm, with minicomputers and personal computers scattered about, although increasingly still chained to corporate data centers if the enterprise was still fundamentally a centralized command-and-control-driven structure. A culture of centralized control existed more often than not in large and mid-size corporations at the time. Information was used to control existing, often stable work from the 1870s to at least 1990. When a firm or an industry began to experience fundamental changes, perhaps beginning in the 1970s (particularly after the two oil crises of that decade) or the 1980s, management increasingly shared and collected information in a dispersed manner so as to continue monitoring and controlling activities, simultaneously using it to analyze patterns of behavior of products and markets.

Note the patterns: Control was followed by analytical use of data, but neither displaced the other. Information moved into more modular yet interconnected groupings as organizations flattened and became more modular and distributed. As organizations sought to reduce layers of management, responsibility for collecting and using information was distributed to ever-lower levels. As a result, blue-collar employees on a shop floor or in a store used computer-presented data to make decisions to build or buy—decisions that in earlier years would have been made by their supervisors using that same (or less) information. Before the 1990s, in general one could say that most of the information a firm used was collected, used, and protected by employees of that firm, that information was expensive to acquire and manage, and that there were few or no benchmarks on how best to manage data. Requirements for information and their growing amounts grew so rapidly in the previous 100 years that there had been little time to organize the process, although superb examples of effective management of data existed across the world's economy. As computers were adopted, bringing with them the requirement to manage data and technology in more disciplined ways, management began to manage information in the ways described in earlier chapters.

One additional trend has stimulated the desire to exercise control, hence increasing the desire for information with which to do that: growth in the size and complexity of enterprises. This is not the place to write a history of that increase in size and complexity, it is, however, relevant to point out that the ten largest private enterprises in the world in 2010 cumulatively employed about 8.9 million people. (Wal-Mart had the largest number: 2.1 million.) These companies were in various industries: retail, petroleum, utilities, manufacturing, telecommunications, and banking. With more than a million employees each, Wal-Mart, China National Petroleum, and State Grid of China employed more people than lived in many countries. Firms employing half a million people are increasingly also becoming common, with more than a dozen in that category.

The smallest of the top 50 companies in the private sector (Daimler) had 256,000 employees. these large organizations do not even account for employment by governments, which in many cases have even more workers, more complexity of organization, and broader arrays of duties. The point here is that these organizations (both private and public) are large, growing, complex enterprises that will need more, not less, information. Each is already an extensive user of information in many forms.

The New Way: Flat and Dispersed

In the late 1980s, the structure of the modern corporation began to change rapidly. Instead of the usual ten or more layers of management, executives aspired to have four to six. Middle managers, which had emerged in the preceding 100 years as conduits of information, were replaced by computers and by better informed lower-level employees. Supply chains matured during this period, business partners joined the corporate ecosystem, and by the early 1990s many functions of a firm were outsourced, along with the sharing of associated information. These changes led to specialization, to economies of scale, and to yet more formalized expectations and monitoring of the various participants in a firm's business environment. Reuse and sharing of resources, including information, became common. For example, a major automotive company would make access to its database records available to business partners who shared responsibility with the larger firm in deciding what components to design, build, and ship. There were complaints of "loss of control" over operations, but in fact the problem was often a loss of control of data and of decisions based on those data. Decisions often were being made by individuals who in earlier times would have done so within the confines of their business "silos," where they controlled all functions rather than relying on business partners to do their part. Trans-organizational dependencies grew as a result. Controls had to give way to increased collaboration.

In the 1990s, collecting information on monitored activities, and analysis of the cost and risks of optional strategies for distributing and outsourcing work became extremely attractive. The "quality management" movement was in full swing, and statistical process-control data were in fashion. Both movements made "reengineering the corporation" possible. Work was seen as becoming more intelligent. Expertise now was situated lower in the enterprise. Managers knew less about how things worked than their employees, even to the extent of sometimes not knowing how to access online information. "Empowerment" and "delegation" became managerial buzzwords. Information continued to be distributed, yet tied to various sources of data that remained centralized in the hands of senior managers. Data was presented in ways that could make the information interactive, that is to say, as a tool to control processes, model options, and direct the work of a firm.

The wide adoption of the Internet as a channel for delivering information by the late 1990s signaled another step change in the role of information. Ways of organizing information took on many of the characteristics of data management similar to those evident in technical communities, such as computer scientists, often embracing their language. New computer architectures were supposed to lead to new information architectures. Internet-scale data centers held out the possibilities of larger sets of data housed in centralized machines and departments, with these larger data sets linked, however, quite intimately with ever-larger "communities of practice" (experts sharing the same data regardless of where people and data were physically located), with additional inflow of information from other sources and organizations. "Throughput," a term used by computer scientists to mean how fast data could be processed in and through a system, became a concern for the modern enterprise.

By the early 2000s, line management and IT experts were increasingly focused on a combination of managerial practices for information and in development of software and hardware. Real-time processing of information became the desired minimal standard of data acquisition and availability, with a growing desire to have that occur continuously. What had been called "sub-second" response times in the 1980s were more clinically called "millisecond" response times, and now had to include analysis of the data at the same time. Unstructured data about the environment, people, and machines became increasingly essential. Work in many parts of the enterprise involved the collection, storage, and analysis of high volumes of data streams, such as the data that comes out of sensors and video, stock quotations and news reports. High volumes of data streams are appearing in organizations of all kinds, but most notably in government, health care, manufacturing, finance, and retail. Injected into this new world are sets of data collected using earlier techniques implemented in enterprise resource planning (ERP) and supply-chain processes. This approach was used since processes and the management of activities embedded in processes remained how work was still organized and optimized.

This is a world still under construction. Consider as an example the speed with which people want information. Knowing within minutes where a fleet of trucks or airplanes was good enough in the early 1980s, but by 1990 people wanted the same data in a second or less. Then, as technology became more accommodating, delivery times started moving to 100 milliseconds, then to 10 milliseconds, and so it continues. Financial systems, continuous process and manufacturing systems, and even call centers had to be monitored, with events reported at the speed with which they occurred.

Today various philosophies about information are emerging. For example, the "open source" movement, which in the 1980s began to make software more widely available, often with no purchase or user fees, became part of a much larger conversation about individuals donating information (as in the case of Wikipedia), having services open to whoever desired access to these (such as to programmers wanting software, or citizens accessing government sponsored information), and led to today's managerial policies and debates on what should be "open" and "closed" types of information. Less critical data sets tended to be offered first in an open environment with copyrighted materials less so, as occurred in the music industry when it resisted free downloading of music by students in the early 2000s.

In the early years of the new century, information in the modern enterprise continued evolving as part of changes in how firms did their work. Outsourcing began evolving into offshoring, with work shifting from one country to another, either to other employees in a company or to closely linked partners. IT-mediated applications facilitated this process, of course, but so did the widespread use of standardized processes that emerged out of process-management initiatives of the 1980s and the 1990s. This all happened in the face of an ever-globalizing business environment.

Networks of information continued to diffuse with all manner and complexity of data. Services within a firm, or as a service to clients, were integrated globally in an increasing fashion. For example, a consultant sells some work in Germany, but the tasks of the project are spread to India and China, and controlled out of several other countries. Work increasingly is organized so that it is scalable, that is to say, can be expanded or reduced in volume or scope, people added or eliminated, tasks moved from one place to another, all necessary information expanded or dispersed as needed, and all these tasks done in a cost-effective manner. This is not theory; it is a widely deployed practice, particularly by the very largest enterprises and their suppliers and business partners.

As the volume of data and information accumulated by man and machine continued to pile up, the possibility of analytics increased too, as evidenced by trends of the past 30 years described above. This use of analytics is driven by newer and more sophisticated software and computational devices. It is also marked by an ever-expanding scientific mindset. To be sure, that mindset began working its way into the modern enterprise by the early 1960s, but with more data one can be more rigorous in their analysis and hence more "scientific" about their use of information. Andrew McAfee of MIT has been making this point for some time, arguing, for instance, that with a great deal of information one could test a business hypothesis before investing money and other resources to a course of action. Part of the challenge for management is to understand what today's analytical software tools can do, but they appreciate the potential benefits of being more analytical in their decision making.

A related behavior that is on the rise is the act of sharing more of one's information in practical ways with the ever-enlarging ecosystem of today's workplace. Increasingly, as security issues are addressed, binding suppliers and customers to a firm using information is becoming normal practice. Surveys done in 2010 by IBM indicated that more than half of the responding firms had or were "piloting" systems to do just that for order taking and status reporting, and for a host of marketing and sales information. Slightly larger percentages of firms are increasing data exchanges with vendors and suppliers across ever-increasing types of data, such as shipping status, tracking, and invoicing, orders placed and their status, and stocking information and POS reports. Less new information is being shared about Web traffic, but that may be because so much is already diffused. Web-based catalogs are now in great demand and represent the next frontier across all industries, with enormous risks because customers can then use software to compare prices, rather than just features and quality. Such information drawn from the Internet could drive away a customer or motivate one to do business with a company that offers more information with their products. Firms have yet to determine how comfortable they should be with customers going to Google for information as opposed to the enterprise's corporate website. So long as various technical standards are used to house and make information available, IT-based comparisons will remain more of a challenge than a reality. But information available from multiple digital sources is a growing part of an enterprise's future.

Integrated Enterprises: The Coming Way

Since the late 1950s, hundreds if not thousands of observers of the modern corporation have been predicting that it would change to reflect the effects of information. The business consultant Peter Drucker was one of the first people to use the term "knowledge management" to describe the role of information. New organizational structures were made possible by information technologies and advances in telecommunications. The forecasts were remarkably quite similar in that they spoke of flatter hierarchies; shared or distributed responsibilities, typically extending the authority of lower level employees; alliances and other forms of collaborative arrangements and partnerships with suppliers and vendors; other alliances and more intimate co-dependent relationships with customers and clients (including outsourcing arrangements); blurred borders between the legal enterprise and an ecosystem of participants in an environment or value chain that could involve multiple companies and non-profit institutions; and firms that straddled industries, playing a role in multiple markets, such as the online bookseller does when it sells things other than books, for instance digital content, music or consumer electronics. In the past 20 years, not a year has gone by without at least a few forecasts being published in book form about the "enterprise of the future," while the *Harvard Business Review*, the *Financial Times*, *The Economist*, and academic business publications routinely speak of the emergence of new structures.

Interest in future forms of the enterprise picked up in the 1990s as truly innovative business models emerged as a direct consequence of what could be done using the Internet, spurring a new wave of forecasts. New types of online companies became symbols of the new possibilities—Amazon, eBay, and Craigslist, to mention a few. These were all born out of the availability of the Internet after it had evolved sufficiently into a vehicle that could handle reasonably secure financial transactions, accept and secure information in various forms from text to video, and became accessible to enough potential customers to make it worthwhile. These new businesses also shared one other thing in common: their main work was managing information about goods and services. Only after they had become successful did some evolve into a more "bricks-and-mortar" operation with physical stores and warehouses. Even those that evolved into a more traditional physical business were exceptions, such as what happened to Amazon when years after it had been established as an online bookseller it built its first warehouse; before that, it moved orders from customers to publishers and distributors to fulfill.

In short, the use of information had profoundly influenced the form and structure of both existing enterprises and those that were anticipated to come. What actually happened is that the modern enterprise evolved into all the forms forecasted, only later and more incrementally than the experts predicted. The modern enterprise is already operating in the form those futurists had described. But it is also still evolving. Surveys done between 2006 and 2010 by the IBM Institute for Business Value, in which more than 10,000 executives all over the world (most of them in *Fortune* 1,000 companies and large government agencies) were interviewed, began to suggest what the next evolutionary events would be. And, as in the past, their views reflected the continuing role of information as the skeletal infrastructure of the firm.

Executives are reporting that they have entered an era characterized by a new round of fundamental changes to their business models, with two-thirds reporting they were refurbishing their organizations and at the same time complaining that one result was that they needed different types of information to support such traditional areas of interest as supply chains and customer relations. Markets are changing, not just simply globalizing (although that too); their employees need different skills, and IT is making new ways of communicating up and down the value chains easier and more frequent to do. These communications are also becoming more integrated into ever smaller work steps. Enterprises are continuing to integrate operations within their expanding business ecosystems, changing the mix of capabilities, information, and assets, deepening relations with partners, and searching for new markets in the growing economies of Asia, Africa, Latin America, and Central and Eastern Europe. There is a surge in activity involving the collection of information about customers, beyond the routine desire to add continuously to insights into operational issues. All these impulses are also being extended to integrate insights at a global level, rather than just by country or division.

Managers speak more often about collaboration among suppliers, regulators, vendors, and customers, arguing that collaborative operational styles are increasingly important in improving efficiencies, dampening competition, and growing closer to customers. To those purposes, information flows play a crucial role for all involved parties. Underpinning their use of information is a less than quiet movement called "corporate social responsibility" (CSR). Customers increasingly want to do business with firms that are reducing their carbon footprint, are ethical in their business practices, and are becoming more "green" (that is, reducing pollution and the use of energy or harmful chemicals). About 75 percent of all respondents report they are focused on addressing these new market requirements through various actions, one of which is to collect information about their own situation. For example, they are documenting their carbon footprints and are beginning to require that their suppliers do the same. They are beginning to understand—and to collect data on—how workers in developing economies are paid and treated in the manufacture of products sold in their markets, insisting on more ethical treatment of workers. In short, information on CSR is now one of the fastest-growing areas of interest expressed by the modern enterprise.

As with other information, enterprises are remolding their business strategies. They know that just mimicking the activities and strategies of the rest of their industry does not provide competitive advantages, let alone lead to exceptional growth in revenues and profits. Identifying innovative strategies begins with information consulted in an organized, ever-more-comprehensive manner, followed by familiar methods of analysis, experimentation, and effective execution. Thus, management and employees are collecting information that helps them focus on what value their firms can provide and identify new opportunities they are capable of pursuing, usually quickly.

The historic role of business intelligence in this process continues to grow as this function becomes increasingly capable of collecting and analyzing three classes of information: strategic insight and predictions, better modeling of financial issues, and improved measures and analyses of effectiveness of programs and other activities. Note the shift from just measuring and understanding efficiencies to increased emphasis on effectiveness. Firms want to use such information to align their operations. Participants in their eco-space want to align business plans to leveraged business intelligence to know more and sooner about that environment. They also want to enhance the speed and ease of making changes in what their firms do, routinely referred to today as building flexibility into one's business models or strategies.

Executives report widely to the press that their firms are entering another period of intensified and novel churning. As a by-product, their greatest challenge is in changing the mindsets and attitudes of employees, business partners, and customers to address changing circumstances. To do this they are using information and fact-based arguments and marketing. Corporate cultures are a problem too, but use of information and expanded communications and economic incentives with participants in an ecosystem have historically proved effective in facilitating changes in work habits.

In short, executives around the world are becoming more dependent on information in their efforts to lead sustainable enterprises, with data and insights pointing to specific actions they can take. They are looking for new sources of data and new information that generate insights more appropriate for different (additional) markets and in a cycle of activity in which competition transforms faster than in the past, along with products, services, regulatory activity, and customer activism. These issues are further complicated by events in one part of the world affecting those in another—the interconnected world that executives and subject-matter experts speak about—and thus requiring a more global perspective on and a more global response to business conditions. It is the primary reason for management attempting to further develop the integrated enterprise forecasted for so many years to arrive. Tactical questions asked up and down the organization today concern information:

• What information do we need?

• Where do we get it?

• How can we get it in a cost-effective way?

One of the biggest uncertainties facing managers is the rising tide of consumer activism regarding environmental issues. The amount of information available on the subject, and the specific, highly detailed pieces of relevant data, are expanding rapidly. Corporations are increasing their efforts to collect such data from many new places and in new ways (e.g., data streams generated by sensors and images transmitted by satellites). Furthermore, consumers are rapidly expanding their use of social network, videos, and chat rooms. These three sources of new data are operating in real time 24 hours a day around the world. This is a new world of information for the modern enterprise.

Information-Only Businesses

Many businesses today are not bricks-and-mortar operations with large office towers, warehouses, and factories. Largely thanks to the availability of the Internet as a vehicle for conducting business, a new class of modern enterprises has blossomed, beginning largely in the mid 1990s in the United States. There were upstart firms in many industries, such as online banks, online insurance providers, eBay in sales, Amazon in books and later other forms of merchandise, and almost every type of information service provider: libraries, industry analysts, real estate brokers, financial advisors, news media, record companies, and so on. In addition, bricks-and-mortar firms have almost universally set up online operations to compliment their traditional ways of doing business. But whichever variant of business model one chooses to look at, they all share one universal feature: they are largely about collecting data, doing something with it, and causing themselves or their bricks-and-mortar business partners to respond—for example, to ship a product sold by an online intermediary, such as an online florist.

This new business model has resulted in a heated debate about information and how to convert it into revenue. Two types of data are involved. Since these companies can use software to keep track of who comes to their websites, what they look at there, for how long, and what action they took, they have used that information to sell targeted advertising. It has been such a successful effort that advertisers have moved huge amounts of their budgets to online sites, putting some traditional industries at risk of failure, such as newspapers and magazines, which depend on advertising but can't quantify in detail who looks at specific advertisements, for how long, how often, or whether they take action, such as placing an order or moving from an advertisement to the website of the advertiser. Companies can do that online. It has been perhaps the most disruptive, stunning development in the use of new information to appear in decades.

The second development has been the ability of such firms to track the history of someone's interactions with the firm, which are conducted entirely online. Google, for example, routinely stores every e-mail message and every "click" that takes place through its systems, tracking the interests of people doing searches for information. It uses this information to develop new services, to deliver more targeted advertising, and it is expected to continue expanding use and sale of this kind of information. Amazon uses such information to suggest to its customers other products that might be of interest to them, basing the suggestions on previous searches of its website, such as other books on the same topic that could be of interest to a customer while that individual is still visiting its website. This one function alone has made it possible to sell incrementally without any additional effort on the part of Amazon.

Of course, with both advertising and customer insights, all activities are global in scope. It is no wonder that in a business environment that values information the vast majority of corporations want a presence on the Web and in many instances are encouraging their customers to use it to interact with their firm, from ordering medicines online, to using it to debug problems with products, to distributing more information about their goods and services without having to use live customer-relations personnel. All the while, a firm tracks every aspect of the dialogs and transactions, accumulating data. It uses the data to document patterns of interest and behavior and volumes of transactions. It then applies predictive analytics to anticipate future volumes, problems, opportunities, and interests.

Implications

There are many implications for the next round of changes in the form and structure of the modern enterprise. The addition of CSR information is only one change requiring a response. Adding new types of information to the traditional functions of an enterprise is another. New connections are required among information and its users, such as linking traditional operational data to CSR information to inform management and customers about the environmentally sustainable capabilities of a firm. Learning the cost and potential savings in operational expenses of a firm's "going green" is a new area of management in which there are few insights, best practices, or appreciation for potential business results. One can reasonably expect this area to grow in volume and importance in the next 20 years, if for no other reason than there are already in place regulatory requirements for generating such information and customer insistence that it be made available to them, hence, to the public and competitors.

As new types of information are needed, the modern enterprise is turning to its partners (including tiny suppliers with only a few employees) for similar data. Such data will lead to new ways of optimizing the performance of a business, but management will need to learn how to do that in new domains of interest, such as in environmental areas and in countries in which they have not operated before.

There are challenges, of course, because needed information often has to be collected for the first time and from new sources. One problem is the growing requirement to share information on how to do that and with whom. Often beginning with new information needed for supply chains, firms extend into other areas of the business, expanding out to its partners, as suggested before. Surveys suggest that, although existing operational and economic environmental data are increasing in quality, often those data are not sufficiently timely. Companies are moving toward practices that call for data weekly, daily, and even hourly, but data may come in much more slowly—perhaps only once a month. Even online data are often described as stale. In some subject areas, eight of ten organizations barely know much about their performance, most notably their carbon footprints, and others are struggling to acquire adequate information about what their customers' think about issues of mutual interest.

Though raw data are increasing exponentially in all industries, firms still face the age-old challenge of converting data into relevant information and insights that makes it possible to take actions. To do that, firms are increasingly identifying specific gaps between the information they have and what they think they need. They also are aligning their business strategies with the aspirations of their customers by using facts more than impressions, gut feel, or even earlier experiences (which may no longer be a good indicator, since circumstances may have changed) to suggest the way. And they are increasing the breadth of their use of such tried and trusted methods of working with data as assessing leading practices and using more benchmarks, and then increasing their use of predictive modeling.

THE FUTURE OF INFORMATION
IN THE MODERN ENTERPRISE

The historic trend over the past 100 years has been for management to increase its dependence on multiple forms of data and information. The development of the computer and subsequently its marriage to communications from data processing to the more complex notions of information technology (IT) and most recently to information and communications technologies (ICT), followed by the availability of the Internet, made it possible to expand the collection, the storage, and the use of data and information. That historic process is continuing to evolve into systems of information that are creating new forms of insight and leading to increased knowledge relevant to the current conditions of a firm. Management is applying more scientifically rigorous methods to the study of data and information, and is shifting to analytical techniques that also project into the future both trends and realistically possible scenarios. By-products of these efforts are recommendations. Such activities are increasingly being done by software empowered to analyze and to take actions. Non-human participants—machines and sensors—are rapidly coming to outnumber the humans who collected and analyzed data as recently as 30 years ago. Though knowledge and wisdom have not been automated, and will not be for some time, many of the steps that precede creation of knowledge and wisdom have been.

This chapter identifies some of the emerging trends and suggests what management can be expected to do in the future enterprise. It will be a world in which much information is more interconnected than it is today, and in which different types of data and from more disparate sources than are available today will affect each other at much shorter intervals than in the past. This is not about computers taking over, it is about a tremendous increase in the harnessing of information to every activity of the modern enterprise, extending the hope of control that helped launch the telegraph, the telephone, the computer, software, and the Internet, and led to the Information Age. Predicting the future is always a difficult, indeed tenuous, activity; however, since fundamental changes come slower than the hype that surrounds them, the future is arriving in some parts of the global economy and in some industries sooner than in others, as was always the case. That is why it is possible to look forward with some confidence and to make recommendations.

It will be a world in which much information is more interconnected than it is today, and in which different types of data and from more disparate sources than are available today will affect each other at much shorter intervals than in the past.

How Information Will Change the Work and the Structure of Enterprises

Demographers and economists speak about more than a billion new people joining the middle class in the next few years, achieving literacy, demanding schools, books, and access to information, and then taking jobs in existing and yet-to-be-established firms. Some Chinese banks already have more customers in China than there are people living in North America. There are shoe factories in China with 30,000 employees, about three to four times as many as a firm employs in an American or European manufacturing plant. Big enterprises need large and highly diverse quantities of information. As more people become potential customers, and IT continues to spread, there will be more big firms with many partner firms linked together sharing information all over the world. Emerging markets already have surpassed the older "advanced" economies with their growth rates as measured by traditional metrics that define the shape of a society and its economy. As the world's standard of living continues to rise and, in the process, equalize more around the world, as it had been before the modern era, enterprises will use information to maintain their relative positions in scores of countries. All of that will happen within the working lives of employees who today are just halfway through their careers. These activities and trends underscore two fundamental features of information: it is increasing in volume and in variety of types and forms.

At the start of the twenty-first century, fewer than a billion people could access the Internet, a few years later that all had changed. By 2010, 2 billion routinely surfed the Web. Those individuals were not concentrated largely in two to three dozen countries as in 2000, but were living and working in nearly 200 nations. These people were competing for time on the Internet too with devices pumping data into the Internet to each other. By 2030 there may be more than a trillion devices that have as part or all of their function to create data and transmit data to each other or to enterprises of all sizes. These may include sensors in automobiles and household appliances, cameras, mobile phones, wired roadways, water lines, gas and oil pipelines, even shelves in retail stores. My colleagues think of these as forming an "Internet of things." The implication is that in time many of the managerial issues discussed in this book will concern the role of machines and products in how both objects study issues, make decisions, and take actions on the basis of their own "smart" capabilities independently of humans or in collaboration with them.

Computer chips—transistors and integrated circuits—in which information is housed as it travels from people and devices to other places and persons are increasing in number as well. In the late 1940s, only a few hundred transistors existed. By 2001 there were more than 60 million for every person on Earth. By the end of 2010, there were about a billion per person. Those transistors are carriers of data and information. The economic incentive to use them also expanded, as the cost went from several dollars each during the late 1940s to a 10-millionth of an American cent in 2010. Think back to the mid 1970s, when a hand-held calculator cost $700, then to 2000, when people began to receive calculators as souvenirs at technical conferences.

One can hardly overestimate the importance of the miniaturization of hardware and the attendant software. To go on a tour in another country 20 years ago, one had to take a travel book, and the biggest one a traveler could haul around might have been about 600 pages. Today a flash memory card can make it possible to bring along a bookcase full of travel information and include videos of various countries, all in a device no larger than a canister of lipstick. Information has become portable in huge quantities. Today data can be attached to a storage device the size of an atom, and computer scientists declare boldly that they can miniaturize further using existing technologies. The implication is already understood: people will want to store and access more data, and will press the technology to handle that additional volume as it converts it into information, presents it in ways humans can appreciate (such as graphics and video), and do analytical work to convert raw facts into insights and knowledge.

Miniaturization of hardware and portability of information means more than simply storing data in ever-smaller machines and things. Again it's portability at work. There is an open, obvious revolution underway, and it is so visible that we almost don't see it: mobile telephones are rapidly evolving into the main computer of choice for individuals, particularly in those countries with the lowest standards of living, but also for personal use in the rest of the world, and as yet another digital tool for employees in the modern enterprise. Besides becoming smaller, lighter, and cheaper to acquire and use, they have "smart" functionality. Beginning in the early 2000s, access to uses and specific types of data became practical—sports, general news, driving instructions, merchants various forms of photography, and now thousands of other functions. Before these moved to cell phones, they were accessible only through personal computers (in the 1980s), then through laptop computers (in the 1990s). Even then apps were more generalized, whereas phone apps can be highly specific and very narrow in scope. Already iPads and other e-readers are beginning to compete with cell phones, stimulating demand with their low cost and their portability. As a result, we can expect such devices—cell phones but to a lesser extent e-readers too—to be the digital tools of choice for billions of people for the foreseeable future. They are spreading so fast that enterprises will extend their information networks to those devices, with all the conveniences and problems associated with such a shift, many of which paralleled their experiences with laptops. This follows the long-standing practice of loading information into IT devices.

Surveys of economic and business trends continue to report about accelerated changes over the past 50 years, and many studies have demonstrated that these concerns are borne out by evidence of sped-up activities. There is also an information-centric speeding up that has been underway for decades with no end in sight, namely the ability of computers to perform ever-larger quantities of calculations faster. The declining cost of putting information into computers and "crunching the numbers" encourages even more use of digitized facts and analyses. It is one important reason why people increasingly use computers to do modeling, forecasting, and, of course, analysis, relying on ever-broader sets of issues, as was noted in earlier chapters.

Around 2010, supercomputers made it possible to perform 10^{15} calculations (a petaflop) in a second. The chips used to achieve this speed are the same ones video game consoles have in them, and the computer was managed by the widely used free Linux software. This means that commercial-grade computer chips and off-the-shelf software— not specially designed expensive components—can be lashed together to work at speeds inching closer to that of the human brain. To be sure, it will be years before such operating speeds appear in hand-held devices and other equipment, but the direction is obvious enough. If there is one managerial and operational principle that corporations have collectively embraced enthusiastically since the 1870s, it is a commitment to speed. Sixty years of using digitized forms of information reinforced this adherence to speed in specific ways.

The path forward is clear. There will be a greater reliance on scientific methods in running a business, and these methods will be supported by ever-larger quantities and variety of information.

What Data Networks and IT in General Make Possible

At the risk of overstating the case and appearing to be writing a sci-fi scenario, there are several trends already in evidence that one can expect to expand into new functions as capabilities evolve and costs drop. All of them depend on data becoming facts and information that will be used more often by machines that have computers embedded within them. More routine, dangerous, and precise work will be done by things than by people. We can already see that mechanical labor at work. The U.S. military uses robots to identify and detonate improvised explosive devices hidden in buildings and buried under roads. Sniffing devices are beginning to be used to identify drugs and explosives, although they are not yet at a point where they can replace a well-trained dog. The U.S. Air Force's drones (pilotless aircraft) use more advanced versions of software that children have used for years to "fly" in video games. Robotic devices are now being used (though not widely yet) to perform medical operations that require very small incisions or precision that is beyond the capabilities of a surgeon. All these devices collect vast quantities of data at near-instantaneous speeds, present the information in ways that are relevant to an operator (a soldier, a police officer, an Air Force operator, a doctor), and respond rapidly to human commands. Miniaturization is occurring here too—already some robots are the size of insects.

The next major step in the evolution in these devices will be to extend to them the authority and capability to make decisions on what to do. This already occurs with mundane tasks in such areas as manufacturing, traffic control, and economic analyses. The next step is to allow them to do things that involve life and death, or to commit resources of an enterprise that are legally binding, or have direct consequences to the bottom line. The social, legal, and moral implications of such possibilities are just now starting to be discussed. But while those discussions heat up, information-laden devices will take over additional amounts of human thinking and decision-making roles.

The implications for the modern enterprise are enormously important. For one thing, if such equipment is less expensive to acquire and run than the cost of people's salaries and benefits, or at least more accurate and safer to use, whole areas of mundane or delicate tasks will be shifted to it. As with employees, results achieved by these information machines will be required to be reported back to management. If they are given the ability to model and forecast as mainframe computers can do today, one can even imagine machines reporting their plans, forecasting what they "think" they will get done in a certain period, acquiring materials and supplies they will need, and maybe even producing reports that explain why they could not get something done, much as a sales representative does today when he prepares an elegant PowerPoint presentation to explain why customers did not buy as much as they were supposed to.

To what extent should devices acquire information, do work, and be held responsible for results? This is a broader question. Today owners of devices of all types are held responsible managerially and legally for the actions of their machines. At some point during the second half of the twenty-first century, that may begin to be thought of as a very "retro" twentieth-century notion of responsibility and accountability. Extend the idea a bit and one has to ask what role human beings will play in such an enterprise. Will they focus more on goal setting and strategies, both of which are information-intensive activities, and less on performing tasks of the enterprise? What levels of authority and responsibility become practical, indeed required, in such a scenario? What kind of education and skills will workers need? Will a Chinese shoe factory that today employs 30,000 workers need only several thousand, or maybe none, if a person can "print out" a new pair of shoes at home? What will happen to the thousands of shoe makers who are no longer needed? What will happen to hundreds of millions, if not more than a billion, unneeded workers? Will a society and its firms make enough money to support the unneeded workers and their families? Or will new types of businesses and work emerge?

The last point is not a crazy one. When a society optimizes its work, environment, and aspirations in a harmonious way, workloads actually decline. Anthropologists and historians have clearly established that "primitive" tribal societies had a considerable amount of leisure time. If having free time is a social aspiration, these tribes were far ahead of today's "advanced" societies, which are now relying so extensively on fact-based work and computers. This brings us to the most basic of human considerations: what roles the enterprise and the economic and social ecosystem in which it operates should play in the years to come. Will the enterprise be a servant of society's wishes, or will it still be subservient to shareholders and wedded to an operating philosophy that most values generating profits, revenues, and growth? These are all issues that will be addressed by management and their professional societies in the years to come, for the simple reason that IT and, more importantly, information will make these and many other options possible, indeed probable.

Working in the Years to Come

How will we work in the next few decades? Experience with our growing reliance on information suggests several possible answers.

First, employees at all levels of an enterprise will increasingly ask and be required to answer that question as part of their normal work. Position on the corporate ladder, though remaining very important, will be determined increasingly by the power individuals have in molding and harnessing information into ways that offer new economic and social advantages, and products and services. In short, the tacit ability to "connect the dots" will be more of a developed, and essential, skill for future workers.

Second, the ability to work with information-laden software and machines will be essential. Generational shifts in skills are already evident, such as the fact that people over the age of 60 do not text very much, while it seems everyone between the ages of 10 and 50 does now. Generational divides in the use of information will not be defined just by such traditional means as shared political experience, taste in music, and so forth. Workers will have to be able to work with many of the new information-handling devices and uses that become available. Management will want to monitor these new uses in a routine fashion as part of their daily work so that these can be integrated into the operation of the enterprise in a timely and cost-effective manner, as they have had to do over the past 100 years with other data-laden devices and ways of doing work.

Third, futurists like to predict that life will be better, cleaner, and less stressful. Some of those things will happen, because already that has been the pattern of human evolution for more than 200 years. But other unforeseen problems will also appear. However, people still like to work and spend long hours on activities that interest them, and will use every form of new information and information-handling tool that comes along for both good and evil purposes and in support of personal interests. For the worker it will be a question of keeping up with such developments to be effective as an employee and leader within the enterprise. Workers will have to be students of information, its supporting technologies, and trends in their industries and areas of interest apart from their regular assigned duties in their firms. For management consultants and professors this is already a way of life. An American military officer routinely spends at least 25 percent of his career undergoing formal education and training. These kinds of practices will extend across larger classes of workers and industries with or without the support of senior management. In short, everyone will be a "knowledge worker."

How Fast and How Slow: Viewing Rates of Change and Enduring Practices

Corporations and their senior managers have valued speed of execution for more than 100 years because fast turnaround makes it possible to squeeze out a competitor, get to market sooner with a product, and reduce the amount of time products remain in inventory, hence their cost and other assets that otherwise are not converted into revenue. Inventory turnovers, for example, have been some of the most time-honored measures of sales used by manufacturers, wholesalers, and retailers. In periods of technological or economic transformations, management is always quick to complain that keeping up with so much change is dangerous and difficult. When those in management are driving change, they like it; when others are doing the pushing, they do not. Organized knowledge about the role of speed in change is not a thoroughly studied subject, although change itself has been examined quite extensively. One can clock changes in an economy (e.g., from agricultural to manufacturing and then to services) by tracking the changes in gross domestic product in each industry or sector, the number of people employed in each, and so forth. However, the speed with which change occurs with information, knowledge, and, just as importantly, work in a corporation remains insufficiently understood. This is not the same as how much new information is added, because new facts do not necessarily force old data to go away.

Anecdotal evidence, however, has led to some "rules of the road" that members of a firm and their industries as a whole should learn and assimilate in the absence of empirical evidence of how rapidly things turn over in a certain part of the economy. We know that data (facts) appear faster today than ever, if only because sensors and computers on the one hand and people and other machines on the other collect information in fractions of a second. Information now is collected so rapidly that many corporations manage cycles of events by the day or by the week, with fresh data, rather than by the month or the quarter as in previous decades. In the 1970s, when I was a salesman for IBM, I would sit down with my manager once a month to review my forecasts and to discuss what was on order and so forth; that was how things were done at all levels of the firm, and it proved to be sound business practice. By the mid 1990s, such reviews were held weekly in all sales organizations and up and down the hierarchy, and the data going into those reviews had changed enough since the preceding week to justify the fourfold reduction in the cycle time for such meetings. Sam Walton of Wal-Mart reviewed sales daily by the mid 1980s, and his computer systems were able to keep up with his demand for daily information, pulling together data from across the firm.

Anecdotal evidence suggests that responses to changes in information have sped up too. For example, in the summer of 2010, Barnes & Noble announced a substantial decrease in the price of its electronic reading device, the Nook, at the start of a business day. The news media picked up the story, and by late morning it seemed the whole world knew of the change. By early afternoon, Amazon—Barnes & Noble's archrival in the market for such devices—had announced a deep cut in the price of its competing product, the Kindle. Between the morning and afternoon announcements, Amazon's management had to (a) understand what was going on, (b) run quantitative models and scenarios on what different prices would do to the firm's financial and revenue prospects, and (c) make decisions that could cost them lost or gained sales. By early afternoon, the press was commenting on the day's events in the market for reading devices, and stock analysts in other countries were reacting while Barnes & Noble and Amazon executives slept.

The closer information is to being data, the faster it comes and goes, or adds up. The more it is like knowledge and wisdom, the slower it changes. Institutional knowledge—and memory—has never been well measured, and our understanding of its dynamics remains uneven. But it is often seen as moving at a very slow pace, indeed so slow that observers have commented on how corporations often fail to respond to changes quickly enough even to avoid going out of business. Wisdom—insight—takes years to accumulate, and the accumulation of wisdom is one of those human activities in which more is better. Adding newer pieces of data to older information leads to pattern recognition and makes better predictions possible. Thus, slowness can be good. What is missing is a set of "rules of the road." For example, does engineering and medical information turn over every four years, as is often stated? Experience (wisdom) would say No, since the laws of physics and mathematics are not so often abrogated in wholesale fashion by new information. On the other hand, we know that corporate marketing campaigns are supplanted every two years or so as market and consumer tastes change. Insights about the next generation of computer chips come in bursts of about two years in length, which is one reason why new computer chips are routinely expected every 18–24 months; indeed, there is even a quasi-rule about this—Moore's Law.

The problem is complicated by the fact that with so many types of information entering the firm that the speed with which it does varies by type even within the enterprise from one department to another. Almost universally, however, surveys on the nature of change regarding the modern enterprise point out that events are generally occurring faster today than before. Since mastering information now is an essential activity for all workers, employees need to be sensitive to the speed with which data, information, knowledge, and wisdom emerge and not simply be experts on the content (data).

Employees will increasingly have to incorporate several activities into the normal cadence of their work and careers, regardless of their role and stature in the enterprise. Indeed, they should do so now.

First, they will increasingly need to rely on organized fact-based activities and decision making, routinely collecting data that can be converted into decision-making insights. That effort has to be methodical (scientific, not just statistical) and has to be ingrained in all important functions. For new topics the issues will remain, as in past years, on counting the number of specific events, then tracking trends as the number of data points collected increase in volume and are cataloged by days, weeks, and quarters. Eventually corporations will reach a point where outcomes and consequences from these collections of data will be documented and analyzed in considerable detail.

Second, the hunt for best practices and comparative rankings and data with other enterprises and institutions will become an even more important part of the work of the enterprise. Managers (including executives), in particular, will have to become students of what other enterprises and departments are doing with their collections of data and their use of information. They will also learn about the activities of other firms by reading reports and external publications, by attending conferences and sharing their own findings, and by talking to individuals inside and outside their firms. All of these activities will concern ever-wider issues, including those that influence their performance in the broader social and economic ecosystem in which they live.

Third, knowledge management and other forms of information management will become more prevalent as managerial practices used by firms to manage their data assets, and will include formal audits, even perhaps operating under the control of legal regulations, and conforming to guidelines of accrediting associations which will require certain information practices. The next twenty years ahead will see an enormous increase in the development of new tools and methods for managing greatly enhanced volumes of data pouring in from machines and sensors—a process that is already underway, though underreported and underappreciated. The management of information as both jobs and careers will probably evolve into more vibrant forms. Today these jobs are largely IT functions; in years to come, information management positions will exist in multiple parts of the enterprise, not just in IT or corporate libraries. The earliest participants in this new wave of work will be those who today have accidentally acquired a disciplined view of information and its management.

Fourth, the world will seem to continue becoming more linked together in what can casually be described as massively more complex supply chains. Thus, employees in the future will have to know how to collect information, work with it, and share it with organizations beyond the legal boundaries of their enterprise. That circumstance will affect legal practices, managerial and operational behaviors, competition, how customers are attracted and retained, and the economic and social contours of societies. These changes will most notably affect the activities in cities where already more than half the population lives and to which political power and authority is flowing and away from state and national regimes.

Some Final Thoughts

Information is the glue that held large and mid-size organizations together for more than 100 years as the First Industrial Revolution gave way to the Second Industrial Revolution, the latter introducing the world to electricity, computers, widespread literacy, education, and communications and transportation technologies. Products, people, and services were wrapped in large swaths of information with no evidence of this influx of information slowing. This trend is not simply the story about the spread of computer technology. It is more substantive, because it concerns the growing reliance of enterprises on data, information, wisdom, and actionable insights intended to generate revenues and profits, and along the way, new products and services derived from information and the disciplined tasks it spawns.

Never has the world of business had such a large number of employees who are literate, educated, and trained formally in business practices. The percentage of managers in corporations who have Masters in Business Administration degrees from universities is higher today than at any time in the past 100 years. Business operations and management became a formal field of study in the twentieth century. We are now entering a period in which the academic, scientific, and practical study of business is expanding in content and through application. In short, the topic has come into its own, much as physics and engineering did in the nineteenth century and mathematics and astronomy in the twentieth. The coming of age of business as a field of knowledge during the second half of the twentieth century ensures that information of many kinds will be studied and applied to a greater extent than it has so far.

This short book on the role of information in the modern enterprise may leave the impression that the use of data and fact-based insights are inevitable. To be sure, the adoption of information-handling practices has been fraught with opportunities and problems, and is still embryonic in its approaches. That will change, of course, as we learn more about how to use information from business schools, from professional associations, from scientists studying the human mind, and from the computer scientists and engineers who are continuously developing new IT, devices, sensors, and software.

Enterprises will continue to become more extensive information-centric organizations, as is happening in ever-expanding sectors of modern society around the world, because people will choose to use information to conquer uncertainty and to mitigate risks in exchange for revenues and profits.

FOR FURTHER INFORMATION

Aspray, William, and Paul Ceruzzi, eds., *The Internet and American Business* (MIT Press, 2008). Provocative and interesting essays, more about the role of information than about the Internet.

Atwood, Christee, *Knowledge Management Basics* (ASTD Press, 2009). A short, practical introduction to the subject; includes practical applications.

Baker, Stephen, *The Numerati* (Houghton Mifflin, 2008). Describes how modeling and forecasting are widely used today by businesses and governments and in higher education.

Blanchard, David, *Supply Chain Management Best Practices* (Wiley, 2010). A good overview of modern supply chains.

Dalkir, Kimiz, *Knowledge Management in Theory and Practice*, second edition (MIT Press, 2011). An excellent resource on knowledge management for practitioners as well as students. Covers all major theories.

Davenport, Thomas, Jeanne Harris, and Robert Morrison, *Analytics at Work: Smarter Decision, Better Results* (Harvard Business School Press, 2010). Experts on analytics and process management describe strategies and provide case studies on the modern use of analytics.

Florida, Richard, *Who's Your City?* (Basic Books, 2008). A sociologist discusses how knowledge workers live and do business.

George, Michael., David Rowlands, and Bill Kastle, *What Is Six Sigma?* (McGraw-Hill, 2003). A good short introduction to the concept as it applies to corporations.

Gleick, James, *The Information: A History, A Theory, A Flood* (Pantheon Books, 2011). Describes how information became the most distinguishing feature of modern society.

Hislop, Donald, *Knowledge Management in Organizations* (Oxford University Press, 2009). Heavy on the theoretical institutional ideas of knowledge at work, but essential if you are going to dig deeply into the topic.

Hugos, Michael, *Essentials of Supply Chain Management*, second edition (Wiley, 2006). A good introduction to the topic. Puts the use of information technology into the broader frameworks of structured supply chains.

Kelly, Kevin, *What Technology Wants* (Viking, 2010). Argues that technologies—including those of information—make up a living neural system in organizations and societies.

Moffitt, Sean, and Mike Dover, *Wiki Brands: Reinventing Your Company in a Customer-Driven Marketplace* (McGraw-Hill, 2011). Describes information-driven marketing strategies in the modern enterprise.

Pyzdek, Thomas, and Paul Keller, *The Six Sigma Handbook* (McGraw-Hill, 2009). An industrial-sized book on how to apply metrics using Six Sigma and other statistical methods.

Qualman, Erik, *Socialnomics: How Social Media Transforms the Way We Live and Do Business* (Wiley, 2009). A marketing executive describes how information moves from and to customers and enterprises today.

Redman, Thomas, *Data Driven: Profiting from Your Most Important Business Asset* (Harvard Business School Press, 2008). A codification of best practices in the use of information with corporations.

Watts, Duncan, *Six Degrees: The Science of a Connected Age* (Norton, 2003). Explains how the world is moving from being focused on things made of atoms to things that are digital.

Wilson, Lonnie, *How to Implement Lean Manufacturing* (McGraw-Hill, 2009). Focuses on the information needed to manage large parts of manufacturing processes.

analytics
The expanded, systematic use of data and related business insights developed through applied analytical disciplines, including statistics, contextual analysis, and quantitative, predictive, and cognitive practices.

best practices
Activities, policies, and processes that are considered superior by multiple firms and are adopted, usually in modified fashion, by other firms.

chief information officer (CIO)
Typically the most senior executive with direct responsibility for running a firm's information technology operations. The CIO may select new uses for computers in the firm, expand access to the Internet within the firm, and help the firm develop business strategies that apply information technologies.

cloud computing
The use of computer applications housed in other departments or divisions, or even outside a firm, on a shared computer system. Often the applications are accessed by means of the Internet.

community of practice (CoP)
Subject-matter experts who work within a firm, often in different departments, but who know one another, collaborate, and typically meet regularly to share information and to train one another.

customer relations management (CRM)
1. Processes for maintaining relations and contacts with customers. 2. A set of processes used to collect information about what customers think of a firm's services and products, and to identify what other services and products they want.

data
Facts obtained by taking measurements or making counts and presented in descriptive, numeric, or graphical forms. When presented in an ordered format that makes them usable, data become information.

ecosystem
In corporate usage, the idea that a firm operates in an environment that is bigger than its own legal borders, with suppliers, business partners, influencers (e.g., regulators and analysts), and customers all interacting. It is an acknowledgment that a firm must acknowledge, manage, and work with the influence of these diverse groups.

enterprise resource planning (ERP) products
Commercially available software products that allow firms to plan and document their financial systems and to plan the allocation of their resources.

explicit knowledge
Understanding of a situation based on specific data, such as numbers, facts, names, and events.

information
Numbers, words, and other data that enable an individual to understand a circumstance. In business these facts provide a context for action and a basis for making decisions.

information and communications technology (ICT)
The combined use of computers and networks (most frequently the Internet).

integrated enterprise
1. A firm that operates across all its divisions, and in all the countries in which it has a presence, in an integrated fashion—for example, by using the same software system for all procurements. 2. A firm that can provide integrated services to other large global firms.

intranet
A communications network that operates within an organization and is accessible only to employees. It relies on the same technologies as the Internet.

knowledge
The collection of understanding, facts, and experiences that can be brought to bear on a situation. Knowledge is used to gain insight into circumstances that sterile statistics or isolated facts might not provide.

knowledge management (KM)
A body of management practices for the collection and use of information in business, science, and government.

line managers
Managers who are on the lowest rungs of the corporate ladder, and/or those who have direct contact with customers. It can also refer to the managers of those managers, most often vice presidents of sales.

pipeline report
A report that describes activities or things currently being worked on in various stages.

process
A collection of activities that takes inputs, transforms them, adds value to them, then delivers an output to an employee, a department, or a customer. A process has a distinct beginning, a series of documented steps, and an end. Best practices call for processes to be defined, repeatable, predictable, and measurable.

radio-frequency identification (RFID)
The use of radio waves to exchange data between a reader and a computer. RFID tags are often put on merchandise to prevent shoplifting and to track inventory.

sensors
Devices that measure activities, such as a weather thermometer or a device used to determine how many cars travel on a certain road.

service chain
A collection of service tasks, such as cooking in a chain of restaurants or repairing automobiles in a network of car dealers.

Six Sigma
A popular measure of performance in business activities (3.4 defects, errors, or failures per million occurrences or performances), used to improve the quality of products and services.

subject-matter expert (SME)
A recognized expert on a topic within a firm or some other organization. People are recognized as SMEs not because of their rank or their work responsibilities but because of their expertise.

supply chain
The coordinated set of activities necessary to develop and deliver a goods or a service.

tacit knowledge
Implicit knowledge—information in a general form (in contrast with facts, numbers, and other explicit data). It is kept in one's mind, not necessarily expressed in words, and acted upon instinctively in a subconscious process of bringing together seemingly unrelated information.

value chain
The chain of activities and processes by which value is added to inputs.

INDEX